LESSONS IN SPIRITUAL DEVELOPMENT

LESSONS IN SPIRITUAL DEVELOPMENT

Insights from Christian-ethos Schools

Ann Casson, Trevor Cooling and Leslie J. Francis

CHURCH HOUSE
PUBLISHING

In association with

Published in 2017 by
Church House Publishing
Church House, Great Smith Street
London SW1P 3AZ.

978 1 7814 0034 0

British Library Cataloguing in Publication Data.
A catalogue record for this book is available from the British Library.
Printed in the United Kingdom by CPI Group (UK) Ltd

Contents

Acknowledgements

This book would not have been possible without the fruitful partnership and collaboration between the research teams of Canterbury Christ Church University, the University of Warwick, and students and staff at the Ten Leading Schools.

We would like to thank all the participants* in the Ten Leading Schools research study for the hospitality and warm welcome they provided the research team, and for all their contributions, in particular those of the students and staff who actively participated in the research process.

We are especially grateful for the support and time given by the principals, head teachers and the key personnel in all the Ten Leading Schools listed below:

- Abbey Grange Church of England Academy, Leeds

- Archbishop Tenison's CE (Church of England) High School, Croydon

- Bishop Justus Church of England School, Bromley

- Bishop Luffa School (a Church of England Teaching School), Chichester

- The Blue Coat School (a Church of England Academy), Oldham

- The John Wallis Church of England Academy, Ashford

- Nottingham Emmanuel School (Church of England), Nottingham

- Oasis Academy, Coulsdon

- St Joseph's Catholic and Anglican High School, Wrexham

- St Mary Redcliffe and Temple School (Church of England), Bristol

Thanks are due to all members of the research teams at the National Institute for Christian Education Research (NICER) at Canterbury Christ Church University, Professor Trevor Cooling, Dr Ann Casson and Elizabeth Melville, and at the Warwick Religions and Education Research Unit (WRERU) at the University of Warwick, Professor Leslie J. Francis and Dr Ursula McKenna.

We would like to thank Dr Beth Green, whose critical insights throughout the project have been invaluable, Dr Gemma Penny and Professor Mark Pike for their support and involvement in the early stages of this research and David Pickering for his careful editorial work. We are grateful to Bishop Stephen for supplying us with his Foreword.

Sincere gratitude is expressed to The Douglas Trust for the funding and invaluable support of the Ten Leading Schools research study.

The names of all participants in this research have been anonymised and pseudonyms used where necessary to ensure confidentiality.

Foreword

The Church of England vision for education promotes the spiritual, physical, intellectual, emotional, moral and social development of children and young people. The vision has the promise by Jesus of 'life in all its fullness' at its heart as we offer a vision of human flourishing for all, one that embraces excellence and academic rigour, but sets them in a wider framework.

Too often in education we allow a false dichotomy to prevail that sets the pursuit of academic rigour against the need to pay attention to the well-being of children and young people. However, we are unequivocal in our message that there is no such distinction – a good education must promote life in all its fullness.

In this book, we find ten examples of jewels in the education system which careful investigation has revealed to be shining examples of what this rounded vision for education can become when it is developed and lived out in the context of a local community and championed by school leaders who are determined to offer something richer and deeper than the often utilitarian approach to education that pervades much of twenty-first century thinking.

It is relatively easy for schools to list a set of values which they aspire to, but these schools demonstrate what can be achieved when those values go beyond any slogan or mission statement and become the daily virtues lived out in the life and character of a school, running through its core like writing through a stick of rock.

Each school studied reveals, in its own way, a crucial aspect of what spiritual development can mean in the context of public education. The combined learning from all ten schools offers an inspiring account of schools motivated by Christian faith and is in stark contrast to the way such schools are often wrongly portrayed by those who have not had an opportunity to find out more about the quality of education provided.

We know that parents who send their child to a school formed around our vision are not disappointed and the evidence from those who have been involved in these ten leading schools confirms why this is the case.

Every chapter bears careful study as the reader is given a glimpse into the life of the school discussed, and the concluding chapters draw the learning together with thoughtful challenge. All those seeking to promote an education that leads to the flourishing of our nation's children and young people will be enriched by the stories of these ten leading schools.

The Rt Revd Stephen Conway

Bishop of Ely and Chair of Church of England Board of Education

Introduction

The crisis of spiritual development

Spiritual development has been present in the language of secondary schools for many years now. In England it became part of the inspection process in the 1990s. Despite that history, there is still significant confusion as to what exactly is meant by the term. It clearly identifies an important area of education, because who would want a spirit-less education in modern schools? However, the danger is that the lack of clarity threatens the whole notion, particularly in a culture where pupils arriving in secondary schools at the age of 11 are being set targets for their performance in GCSE public examinations at the age of 16 and spend the next five years being tracked against those targets. The data of performance can drown what aspiration a school might have to give attention to the spiritual life of its pupils. It just feels too fluffy in an age when accountability to hard data is king.

There is another challenge exacerbating this lack of clarity surrounding spiritual development. Too often the term is used to duck the controversial question of the contribution of the so-called faith schools, of which there are growing numbers in Britain. Current society is so tense about the 'religious question' that many teachers feel uncomfortable talking about the distinctive contribution that might be made by a Christian or other distinctively religious school. The question is, how can we legitimately promote spiritual development in a Christian or other religious school when some, possibly most, pupils are not themselves Christian or from Christian backgrounds? So we revert to the language of the spiritual in the hope that it will be more inclusive and appear less sectarian and abandon the concept of distinctively religious insights. But what then do the religious ethos schools contribute? Certainly the main provider of state-funded church schools in England, namely the Church of England, aspires that its schools should offer an education that is 'deeply Christian' in the cause of 'serving the common good'. If this is to happen, more clarity is needed.

The Ten Leading Schools project is a joint initiative between the National Institute for Christian Education Research (NICER) at Canterbury Christ Church University and the Warwick Religions and Education Research Unit (WRERU) at the University of Warwick and seeks to contribute some helpful insights into this confused landscape. The aspiration is to offer models of spiritual development from actual Christian-ethos secondary schools from England and Wales rather than to engage in theoretical analysis. Our aim is to highlight the features of these schools that contribute to positive spiritual development for pupils. This book offers these insights in a form that we hope will be of practical use for other secondary schools.

The Ten Leading Schools project

In order to achieve this goal, the project steering group recruited ten leading Christian-ethos secondary schools. There is no hard data that ranks schools for spiritual development, and by 'leading' we most certainly did not mean schools that were at the top of some spiritual league table. Rather, we meant schools that stood out because of the care and attention they gave to promoting spiritual development. By Christian-ethos schools we meant schools that sought to do this in a way that was rooted in the Christian scriptures. In order to find these schools, we ran a nationwide competition, inviting applications from schools that wished to participate in the project and advertising five selection criteria against which the applications would be judged. From the applications received, ten were selected; eight were Church of England schools, one was a joint Anglican–Catholic school and one was a member of Oasis Community Learning, a major multi-academy trust. Remarkably, all ten were totally faithful and stayed with the project throughout its two-year duration. Most importantly, this research was designed to showcase the work of the schools and each has a chapter devoted to it. This is not a critical or evaluative project. Rather, it is an attempt to share the stories of ten enthusiastic schools. By so doing our prayer is that other schools will be inspired in giving attention to spiritual development. Unusually for a research project, all schools are named, although individual participants are kept anonymous wherever possible.

The project took a mixed-methods approach, including both qualitative and quantitative data collection. The qualitative work was led by Dr Ann Casson from NICER who spent 12 months criss-crossing the country immersing herself in the life of the ten schools and another 12 months analysing and writing about the massive data-set that she had collected. The quantitative work was led by Professor Leslie J. Francis and Dr Ursula McKenna from WRERU. All schools completed a survey that included the *Francis Scale of Attitude toward Christianity* in both 2015 and 2016. Tasters of the results are given in each school's chapter and a fuller description of the overall data that emerged is given in the appendix.

The mission of Christian-ethos schools

The notion of Christian-ethos schools is a rich and varied concept. This richness and variety is rooted in the Gospel tradition and in Jesus' own strategy for proclaiming and displaying the kingdom of God. Jesus' strategy embraced and combined two distinctive perspectives.

For much of his time Jesus was building up, nurturing and forming a relatively small group of closely bonded followers. These constituted the learning community who came to know him well, who believed in him and who built their lives around him. Among this learning community Jesus was part of the family, eating with Simon Peter's family in Capernaum (Mark 1.29–31) and with Mary and Martha in Bethany (Luke 10.38–42).

At the same time Jesus was also building up, nurturing and shaping a much wider circle of loosely knit followers. These constituted a learning community whose lives were touched by him in a variety of ways. One day 5,000 feasted on five loaves (Mark 6.34–44), and another day 4,000 feasted on seven loaves (Mark 8.1–9). One day crowds were taught on the mountain (Matthew 5.1–7, 28), and another day crowds were taught on level ground (Luke 6.17–49). The wider group experienced the benefits of Jesus' ministry while his close-knit group of disciples grew in faith.

In the Gospel tradition Jesus seemed to move effortlessly between these two situations. In Mark 6 Jesus moves from taking the 12 to one side in the boat directly to feeding the five thousand. In Luke 6 Jesus moved from addressing a large crowd to teaching his disciples. He was concerned with the spiritual development of both groups.

Christian-ethos secondary schools in England and Wales today continue to value these two ministries for their learning communities. A few emphasise working among Christian families while the majority emphasise working among the wider local community. The difference is often seen in their admission policies. The recent Church of England vision statement *Deeply Christian, Serving the Common Good*[1] epitomises how both these aspirations resonate with each other. It develops the aspiration of the 2001 Dearing Report from the Church of England that its schools should offer a spiritual dimension to the lives of all young people who attend. This study of ten leading Christian-ethos secondary schools includes examples of both perspectives and of the range between them.

Researching Christian-ethos schools

Just as the variety of Christian-ethos schools is rooted in the Gospel tradition, so the motivation for researching these schools is rooted in the Gospel tradition. So often when people asked Jesus to teach them about the kingdom of God, he responded by inviting them to go out and to observe what is going on. The Parable of the Sower (Mark 4.1–9) is a prime example of this approach. It is the approach that some of us have characterised as 'empirical theology'.

As empirical theologians, we drew on our best research tools to go and see what is happening in Christian-ethos secondary schools. We were looking for signs of the kingdom of God in our midst. A lot of our research is rooted in the theories and methods of ethnographic studies. Ann Casson spent considerable periods of time in each of the ten schools. She read their documentation; she met the students; she talked with governors, staff and parents; she imbibed the atmosphere.

Another strand of our research is rooted in the theories and methods of quantitative studies. Leslie Francis has spent his life designing surveys and trying to measure the ethos of church schools, beginning with his first serious study in 1974. At the heart of Leslie's work is a concern with measuring what he calls 'attitude toward Christianity'. *The Francis Scale of Attitude toward Christianity* was first published in 1978. It has been translated into over 20 languages and used in over 300 studies.

Attitude toward Christianity is concerned with the affective aspect of religion. It is not concerned with what people believe or about their religious practices. It is concerned with how people feel about religion. In his early studies Leslie argued that it was a legitimate aim for all Christian-ethos schools to promote a positive attitude toward Christianity.

Promoting a positive attitude toward Christianity is not the same thing as indoctrination. It is not setting out to make people believe religious things, or even to do religious things. It is concerned with seeing the potential benefits offered by Christianity.

In the course of our study the *Francis Scale of Attitude toward Christianity* was employed twice. In the first year of the study all students in Years 9 and 10 were invited to complete a survey on attitude toward Christianity and personal values. In the second year of the study all students in Years 7, 8, 9, 10 and 11 were invited to complete a survey on attitude toward Christianity and Christian values.

An overview of the chapters in this book

The core of this book is a collection of case study stories (Chapters 1–10). These paint a picture of ten very different Christian-ethos secondary schools that have prioritised students' spiritual development. Each of the schools has adopted a unique approach, and this overview of these chapters presents a glimpse of the rich diversity of these stories. Each chapter highlights the features that contribute to students' spiritual development in one particular school. The first three case studies (Chapters 1, 2 and 3) are rooted in the concept of hope and aspiration; they explore pastoral care and Christian nurture, promoting Christian values rooted in hope, and empowering students to become leaders and advocates for the vulnerable. The concept of community frames the next two case studies (Chapters 4 and 5), with a focus on the sense of belonging to a Christian community and the ways in which school chaplaincy supports the development of this in school. Chapters 6 and 7 explore the importance for students of being able to question and challenge faith and the benefits of enhancing theological and scriptural literacy in a church school. Promoting Christian values and practices in school are fundamental features in the stories of the two schools in Chapters 8 and 9. The final case study (Chapter 10) considers the contribution of time and space for reflection for students' spiritual development. Chapter 11 considers some of the many implications of this research and, finally, the Appendix provides insights into the quantitative strand of the project.

At the beginning of each chapter, students' responses to five statements drawn from the quantitative survey are shown. This information paints a picture of attitudes to Christianity and the spiritual dimension within the student population of each school. They provide a glimpse into the nature of the student population; they are not a measure of spiritual development, but provide the context for each school's approach to spiritual development. The strength of the research study has been its strategy of listening to the views of the students and staff within the ten schools, and the chapters have been written in such a way so as to give an opportunity for the reader to appreciate as much as possible the insights offered by members of these schools. Each school agreed to be named in this book; however, all quotes from staff and students have been anonymised (pseudonyms have been used when appropriate).

Each chapter can be read independently and will hopefully raise questions among readers about their own practice and/or experience of young people's spiritual development. It is envisaged that this book will be used to stimulate discussion on the contribution that schools can make to young people's spiritual development.

It might be helpful to approach each chapter with the following five questions in mind.

- What are the three most significant things that you will take away from this case study?

- What in this chapter is of particular relevance for your work?

- Has this chapter suggested anything that would make a difference to practice in your school?

- Has anything in this school's approach surprised you or were you expecting something that was not mentioned?

- In what ways can schools support inclusive spiritual development and make a positive contribution to students from a variety of religious and non-religious backgrounds?

Chapter 1 – 'I have come that they may have life, and have it to the full'

The Christian ethos of The John Wallis Academy, Ashford is rooted in the concept that all humans are made in the image of God and all should be able to fulfil their God-given potential. An idea echoed by staff in this academy is that spiritual development is about removing barriers to enable students to access life. For young people to develop fully, barriers do need to be removed, barriers that might be physical, emotional, social and spiritual. This chapter demonstrates how an investment in and prioritising of high-quality effective pastoral care enables these barriers to be breached, if not removed, and facilitates the process for many pupils to fulfil their potential.

Chapter 2 – 'Be the change you wish to see'

Rarely in Christian education is the spotlight shone on the application of Christian social teaching not as a classroom study but in practice. The emphasis on social action in Abbey Grange Church of England Academy, Leeds is built around their motto, 'In partnership to Educate, Nurture and Empower'. In this chapter students articulate how the school has enabled them to understand Christianity as faith in action and to use their talents to become leaders of others in the field of social action and Christian mission.

Chapter 3 – 'The glory of God is a human fully alive'

The Christian imperative to bring hope to others is made visible in St Mary Redcliffe and Temple School, Bristol with a clear strategy and policy of prioritising Christian values and a whole-school commitment to issues of social justice, for example in active partnership with a secondary school in rural Uganda. Such an approach encourages students to develop and to become advocates on behalf of the vulnerable and the disadvantaged in school and in the local, national and international community.

Chapter 4 – 'Educating for life together'

An essential element of spiritual development is that humans develop through being with others; part of a holistic Christian education is educating for 'life together', for living in community. The story of Bishop Justus Church of England School, Bromley centres around the sense of belonging to an inclusive Christian community within school. A consequence of this strong sense of community is that it provides an environment where collective worship flourishes within a community and provides a safe space where students can explore and discuss spiritual matters.

Chapter 5 – 'A faith journey without a map, but with people who give guidance on that journey'

Students in all the Ten Leading Schools were clear that spiritual development is not just about what you believe, but about what you do. The message of Christian service, found in the school motto, 'Together to learn, to grow, to serve', characterised the story of Nottingham Emmanuel School. This chapter considers the role of chaplains in supporting a Christian community within school and the impact of encouraging all students to undertake Christian service in the local and national community.

Chapter 6 – 'A space to challenge, to question and to discover meaning'

The story of The Blue Coat School, Oldham highlights how prioritising inquiry within Religious Education (RE) and collective worship influences spiritual development and enables students to develop an informed spiritual identity. The approach taken by this school focuses on encouraging students to develop a 'questioning and intelligent faith' and this chapter explores how RE and collective worship provide a time and space for students to explore, discuss and reflect, providing a space to discover meaning and to encounter the spiritual dimension of life.

Chapter 7 – 'A questioning, wise and educated faith'

The story of Archbishop Tenison's CE (Church of England) High School, Croydon focuses on promoting theological literacy as a means of stretching and deepening students' understanding of the Christian faith. This school is unique in the group of Ten Leading Schools in so much as the majority of students could draw on a rich experience of the Christian faith from their home background. This chapter considers how a Church of England school contributes to the spiritual development of active young Christians.

Chapter 8 – 'It is about encounter, those Emmaus moments'

Within Christian-ethos secondary schools, spiritual development is framed within a Christian context and the practice of prayer, of being with God, of 'making a connection with God', was important for students in all ten schools. For many staff and students in St Joseph's Catholic and Anglican High School, Wrexham, prayer in a variety of forms is an active and powerful part of school life. This chapter highlights a school where a prayerful culture and Gospel values permeate the whole-school ethos, enabling a healthy community to flourish.

Chapter 9 – 'An inclusive family: a desire to treat everyone equally, respecting differences'

How a Christian-ethos school addresses the needs of the most vulnerable in its community affects not only their ability to develop spiritually, but also provides a role model for the rest of the school community with regard to fundamental Christian values and the understanding of spiritual development in a Christian context. The story of Oasis Academy, Coulsdon demonstrates how one Christian-ethos school prioritises the needs of the most vulnerable, and the influence this approach has on the spiritual development of all students and staff.

Chapter 10 – 'A time for reflection and reconciliation'

A challenge for Christian-ethos schools is how to support students when 'things' are not going well. All schools have to deal with students who challenge the rules of the community, with death within the community, and external events that raise questions about the nature of Christian faith. The story of Bishop Luffa School shows a school that has reflected on these challenges and created space and time in school for reflection, whether in the practice of restorative approaches or in metaphorical and physical space in school.

Chapter 11 considers the implications arising from the research study on which this book is based, highlighting issues such as the importance of context and the contribution that this study makes to current debates in Christian education. Finally, the **Appendix** sets out some of the many findings from the quantitative strand of research exploring students' attitudes to Christianity, providing comparison with a wider data set and highlighting the differences between the ten schools.

Endnote

1. See the vision statement *Deeply Christian, Serving the Common Good*, published in July 2016.

1

Removing barriers to life

Key ideas: pastoral care; Christian role models; aspiration

Students In the John Wallis Academy said:

21%   God is very real to me

21%   I know that Jesus helps me

27%   I believe that God listens to prayers

31%   I am a spiritual person

23%   I am a religious person

THE JOHN WALLIS CHURCH OF ENGLAND ACADEMY, ASHFORD

Coeducational comprehensive school

3–19 years

c.1,530 students

Motto: High Aspirations, High Expectations, High Standards

 The staff were amazing; they just felt like a love bomb.

The nature of the Christian ethos varies from school to school; in some it is more implicit than explicit. In The John Wallis Academy, an ethos visibly rooted in the Christian concepts of care and nurture is encountered the moment you walk through the school gate. It is the breadth and depth of the pastoral care and the compassion that was highlighted by all staff, students and parents. A parent shared with me the many problems she had experienced with her daughter the previous year and suggested that it was only because of the support and compassion of staff at The John Wallis Academy that they both had 'got through it'.

I love being on the gate because I love welcoming the students in in the morning. Even if they are late! (Chaplain)

On a cold January morning in 2015, I stood at the academy gate as the students were welcomed by the chaplain. A simple routine task, yet several staff pointed to this time and this place as when the Christian ethos of the academy was most visible. Listening to the chaplain as he joked, cajoled and wished each student well, the depth of relationships of trust and care was highlighted.

I have come that they may have life, and have it to the full. (John 10.10)

The story of this academy demonstrates the contribution of outstanding pastoral care to students' spiritual development. High-quality pastoral care is effective in removing the barriers to accessing development in all dimensions of life – social, cultural, moral and spiritual. Its influence can also be seen when framed in a Christian context rooted in Christian nurture and supported by prayer. This chapter considers some of the many features that contribute to spiritual development in The John Wallis Academy: the rooting of the pastoral care system in Christian values and practices; the importance of Christian role models, particularly when they are often the only Christian role models that many students will encounter, and the understanding of a Christian duty to raise young people's aspirations in all aspects of life.

Enabling all to live life to the full

The idea of removing barriers to [students'] own social development, spiritual development and learning; it's something that we seem to be quite reasonable at doing. I do think it is almost like a Christian duty, a spiritual duty to remove these barriers. (Staff)

The pastoral care system in The John Wallis Academy was highlighted by staff and students as both reflecting and underpinning the whole Christian ethos of the school. One member of staff described the approach as that of removing barriers to living life in its fullness, barriers that needed to be removed before the young people could access learning. Their removal was essential if the students were to live life to the full, in all its dimensions, including the spiritual. The Christian ethos was exemplified by the varied and extensive work of the pastoral team, extending out to families and into the local community, and it was underpinned by a vision of the raising of expectations and aspirations, enhancing self-worth, boosting self-confidence and self-esteem.

Students recognised that all staff throughout the school had a role in their pastoral care, that they 'care for us'. They identified and appreciated the emphasis that the school put on the Christian values of forgiveness and compassion; teachers were seen as 'not to judge other people', but were there to forgive mistakes and allow 'fresh starts'.

You can tell we're a Christian school by all of our teachers and our relationship in a way, because most things are actually forgiven. (Student)

You have to win [students'] trust and prove that you are going to stay and you aren't going to let them down. You have a huge need for a Christian ethos, for a caring, trusting, respectful work environment. (Staff)

Some of the students in The John Wallis Academy faced immense challenges in accessing education, as the staff explained: some came from 'very deprived backgrounds'; parental attitudes were sometimes not supportive; some lacked a structured home life, had a low sense of self-worth, and were living in a local culture that was not conducive to learning.

The academy's response to this challenge was to seek to ensure that all students should be able to live life to the full (John 10.10).

> **Forgiveness and love unconditionally underpins everything across the Academy ... they know that they are loved.** (Staff)

The pastoral managers interpreted their role in the context of the Christian ethos – an ethos centred in the biblical themes of 'forgiveness and love', arguing that they lived these themes out daily in their work. For example, every conversation was influenced by the concept of forgiveness; they would always begin with the question to both students and families: how can we help you make a fresh start? They would counsel the young people and the families, even if this often meant just sitting, listening and reflecting with them how they could have done things differently. The pastoral managers saw their role as providing the one constant in many students' lives, not as a replacement parent but as a positive role model, a source of the fairness and justice that makes young people feel secure.

Care, nurture and compassion

> **Every time you listen to [the principal] speak, his compassion for the children is unbelievable.** (Parent)

The care and nurture for students expressed in The John Wallis Academy went beyond the norm. Staff pointed out numerous examples, such as all Year 7 being provided with free uniform and a school bag; the chaplain visiting all students in the summer holiday before they started at the academy and, during the school year, paying visits to all students not attending school, for whatever reason. Other examples shared with me included taking food parcels to families and actively seeking support from external agencies to support some of the more vulnerable families in the school holidays.

For the staff working with these students there was a satisfaction that what they were doing was overcoming the barriers to life. They noted that it was often the small things that showed positive influence – the student who turns up on time or the sense of pride when, because of input from the academy, students are able to celebrate at the end of their Year 11 prom. Staff believed that The John Wallis Academy was unique and that in this school you came to realise that your presence was making a difference, whether as the principal, the chaplain, a teacher or a member of the support staff.

> **I want to do it again because it makes you feel good about helping out other people and it makes you feel good about giving back. It's only a bit of your time and it's giving so much to them, it's quite nice to feel you're doing something good for people.** (Student)

The care that staff demonstrated for the students was echoed by the care the students showed for each other and for their local community. The Student Council in the summer of 2015 organised a fair in aid of Kent Air Ambulance. They were motivated to choose this cause because recently a fellow student, having been knocked down by a car and seriously injured, had been picked up by air ambulance.

The students had persuaded the principal to let them organise this summer fair; they spoke about it and promoted it in assemblies and posted leaflets in the local area. The students enthused about their involvement – they had enjoyed taking on the responsibility and had enjoyed the sense of helping other people. The Student Council was led by a member of staff who had done much of the facilitation, but she herself was in awe of the efforts the young people had put in to make it a success for their local community.

> Frankly, I don't know of another school that has had students lead it. Because we don't have a PTA [Parent Teacher Association] it was 100% student effort. (Staff)

The idea was about to do something for the community. We wanted to do it [because] it would benefit other people other than us. It would boost the local economy, business, stuff like that, you know, in our local area. (Student)

When I listened to the students enthuse about their success in raising funds for the air ambulance, it became apparent that they saw themselves as role models for other students. They were demonstrating not only their care for their fellow students, and for others who might need the services of the air ambulance, but also care and concern for their local community which they perceived needed something like a summer fair.

Prayer

Prayer provides a space between the reality of chaos and being involved in the lives of these children, and it creates a space for us to think. (External professional)

The presence of prayer in The John Wallis Academy gave an indication of the Christian roots of this pastoral care. The prayerful culture was often remarked on as a sign of care for the students and for staff; it set the needs of the school community very much within a Christian context. Every meeting, every day, would start with a prayer, a moment of reflection on the task ahead, a focusing in on the particular needs of the students, and often meetings would also end with a prayer.

I could not believe how often people prayed when I came here. The words that people use are so helpful. We need to be able to think and hold in mind the children who we are about to discuss so we can work out the best for them. It provides a small stillness that allows us then to think. (External professional)

Prayer is found at the beginning of day, in assemblies and in tutor times, and there is a 'thought for the day' reflection time every day. The students are exposed to the idea of prayer as being an integral aspect of being a Christian, as an expression of the Christian faith; they are always invited to join in with prayer. As the culture of an acceptance of prayer in The John Wallis Academy has developed, students will seek out people to pray for them; they may wander up to the Religious Education (RE) corridor in their breaks to ask for a prayer for themselves or for a relative or friend, or ask the principal as he crosses the school yard at lunchtime.

> **The children really respond very, very well to the prayer; they actually like it. They're really respectful of prayer, they wouldn't interrupt it.**
> (Staff)

In an RE lesson, the students were tasked with composing a prayer about the stewardship of the world. Several of the students took this as an opportunity to focus on concerns of their own.

- Dear God, help us care for the world and we pray that we can get through the day with no trouble.

- Keep everyone safe and make the world a better place ...

- Dear Lord, can you keep everyone safe. Amen.

- Dear Lord, please help everyone who is having problems and help the school so it is safe, and protect everyone.

> **They are very caring here; when they know it's the right thing, they want to pray. Not always voicing it – it's not aloud, but they will do it in different ways.**
> (Staff)

The small chapel in the academy has become important for students in times of crisis, such as the student's road accident and deaths within the family. Students have used the chapel as a 'place of quietness'. A prayer table had been set up where students can go and write a prayer and leave it in the chapel.

Christian role models

> **I am out to tap into people's spirituality and to say life is more than getting up in the morning, going to do a job and coming back. It is about the meaning of life, who are we, where are we going, that's what it's all about.** (Principal)

> **You are often the only light in that person's life.** (Staff)

The fact that prayer had become so accepted by the students was in a great part down to the modelling of prayer by the members of staff. This highlights the place of Christian role models within the school community. They provide a positive influence on the Christian ethos of the school.

The principal would pray in meetings and in assemblies for members of staff and for students by name; this was drawn to my attention by many staff and students. They interpreted this as a sign that 'he cared'. Prayer was not an abstract concept, but a concrete reality.

My prayer this morning was that we bring the peace, joy and love of Jesus Christ to people every day. That's the unique role that a principal has in a faith school, living out the Gospel values of faith, hope and love. All those are part of my prayer. I always say I am helping to bring your peace and your joy and your love to others every day and then for people to see Christ in you. (Principal)

A key role model in any school is the principal, and the senior leadership; they often set the 'tone' for the school environment. All staff and students in The John Wallis Academy spoke of the influence of their principal on their behaviour and on the ways in which they understood the Christian ethos of the school. For the principal, prayer was an essential element of both being a Christian and being a spiritual leader. He argued that leaders of church schools must be prepared to speak out about faith to lead and to show faith is important. When he met new members of staff, it was made clear to them that the school was a Christian community, and he expected all members of staff to 'respect the prayer life of the school'.

Within The John Wallis Academy, there were many other Christian role models, for example the chaplain, and several staff interpreted their role in school as being a Christian role model for students. The chaplain explained that being a Christian role model had to be taken seriously in The John Wallis Academy. He argued that often you may be the only Christian that students might encounter. In fact, 'many of the students would tell you they don't believe in God', although they often cannot tell you why.

You yourself are the best Bible that some people ever read. So the way I am, the way I conduct myself, the way they see me behaving is probably the only Bible they might pick up, some of them. So it's about mirroring the Gospel values to them. (Chaplain)

The students perceived that most of the staff were Christian, as they were strong about their faith, respectful and eager to pray. Perhaps most tellingly, several of the students emphasised that being a Christian teacher meant they always 'encourage you even when you say I'll give up'. One student concluded that 'it's more like they believe in you more than you do yourself sometimes'. It is interesting that in all ten schools, students often made the assumptions that their teachers were Christian.

Role modelling Christian values and practices is not effective if it is not based on a strong relationship of mutual respect and trust. All members of the school community highlighted how much they valued the relationships in school between staff and students. These relationships were characterised by loyalty, trust, respect and openness to sharing problems and successes, which resulted in a strong sense of belonging and pride in the school community expressed by all.

I am a Christian and I believe that everybody deserves a second chance, a third chance, and God has given me grace and I believe I should treat all students, everybody, the same way. A lot of them are in very hard situations, so it's really sort of helping them to see that they are valued human beings. God loves them as he does all of us. (Staff)

In The John Wallis Academy, it is seen as important to demonstrate that 'we all make mistakes and all need support and help'. The principal argued that he set the example, that he needed to set this example to staff and students. He would admit to them that he made mistakes, and 'say I am really sorry I got that wrong'. He could do that within this community because he prayed with them and it was important that students recognised that he, like everybody in the community, 'was a sinner who needs as much support and help from God as everybody does'.

A teacher shared an example of what he had identified as one of the effects of this role modelling. The previous day he had been on playground duty watching two of the younger pupils throw a ball between each other, but not very successfully. As the ball rolled away yet again, it rolled into the path of a student whose behaviour when he first came to the academy had posed many challenges for staff and other students. The teacher prepared to intervene, but the student 'gently tossed it back to them and they carried on their game and he carried on his way'. The teacher argued that this may not be 'explicitly a spiritual thing', but before the establishment of an explicit Christian ethos and modelling of Christian values this would not have happened.

There is the ethos in the school that is based on prayer, which is based on Christian beliefs; I think that is what allows those kinds of things to then develop.
(Staff)

Another teacher spoke of his work with students who struggled to access 'normal lessons'. He provides an alternative curriculum mainly for those children struggling with specific subjects. It is a structured environment, with clear rules but few sanctions. He aims to rebuild their self-confidence and help them re-access mainstream learning within the academy. He explained that many of the students were in a state of complete 'hopelessness'. They felt that everyone had let them down, including their family and their friends. He saw his role as to try to show them 'that there's more to life' and to let them know that for Christians 'God never lets us down'.

> **Most students suffer from a lack of confidence, despite all the showiness, and the key element to overcome this is the relationship with the young people.** (Staff)

The staff emphasised how important it was to be a positive role model and to provide a consistency of expectation. The students often lacked emotional confidence, and there was a huge need to boost their self-esteem – 'we try to help them to believe in themselves'.

High aspirations

> 'Wow that's great, you've got gifts.' [The John Wallis Academy] suggests that everybody has a gift; people get celebrated for different things. (Parent)

> **Some of the teachers make you feel that you do have a chance of getting into university. I like that. It feels a bit like a family.** (Student)

An important area where the influence of this Christian ethos and role modelling could be seen was in the development of the Christian value of hope and aspiration in the students. The high expectations of the principal, the belief that staff would 'never give up on you', led many of the students to share the aspirations that they had developed since being in The John Wallis Academy.

The students had drawn attention to the principal's 'good' relationship with students. He was approachable, cared for them, and had such high expectations of everyone. However, the characteristic that students highlighted most was that the principal was 'really protective, because he wants his students to be the best'. They were eager to stress that all teachers helped them formulate their 'dreams' and gave them, where possible, the opportunities to achieve them.

> **[The principal] gets on well with the students. You go up to him and he's quite calm and quite funny actually, and not scary.** (Student)

As one student explained, young people in The John Wallis Academy were given chances that she perceived would not be available elsewhere, because of 'their background and stuff'. In The John Wallis Academy it did not matter who you were: the opportunities were given to you. 'They make your dreams come true ... If I said my dream was next week I want to dance, I want to dance in assembly, they'll make it happen.'

> **They will give you the chance. They will give you the equipment or the resources. They probably won't do it for you – they will give you the stuff and let you do it.** (Student)

[The John Wallis Academy] wants the student to be a light to go into the world and then share their light. Like it says in the Bible – Christians share a light. So I think [the principal] is building us up and giving us opportunity to be a light [for others] in life. (Student)

Parents and students highlighted that this hope and aspiration was rooted in the Christian belief that all students should have the opportunity to live life to the full. Living life to the full means giving students the means to develop their God-given gifts. The parents appreciated that the teachers 'believed' in their children and always sought to bring out the best in them.

Students at the academy said:

95%   I want to be successful in life

82%   I have high hopes for my future

88%   I want to do my very best at school

91%   I want to make the most of my life

The focus on removing barriers and raising aspirations that resonates throughout The John Wallis Academy is an important contributor to young people's spiritual development. The challenges of encounters with social and family concerns, difficulties in accessing learning in class, coupled with low self-esteem and confidence for many young people, have to be overcome every day. The John Wallis Academy provides the resources to help students overcome these challenges and creates an environment of Christian care, nurture and expectation of living life to the full in which many young people may flourish.

Chapter overview

- Enabling all to live life to the full
- Care, nurture and compassion
- Prayer
- Christian role models
- High aspirations

2

Developing an empowered community of students

Key ideas: social justice; peer group leaders; Christian cell groups

Students in Abbey Grange Academy said:

50%   God is very real to me

48%   I know that Jesus helps me

53%   I believe that God listens to prayers

40%   I am a spiritual person

52%   I am a religious person

**ABBEY GRANGE CHURCH
OF ENGLAND ACADEMY, LEEDS**

Coeducational comprehensive school

11–18 years

c.1,400 students

Motto: Educate, Nurture and Empower

 Be the change you wish to see in the world.

If you were to spend a day in the small chaplaincy room at the centre of Abbey Grange Church of England Academy or shadow the academy chaplain for a day maybe you, like me, would come to the conclusion that empowering students to be leaders is like dropping a stone into a pond and creating innumerable, unstoppable ripples. The chaplaincy room is a hub of activity. The walls are covered with posters advertising charity fundraising events, this term's programmes for various social justice groups, Fairtrade,[1] Global Justice, and Leeds Citizens;[2] a calendar to book in student events; photos from the annual academy retreat; artwork produced by the five Christian lunchtime groups and some post-it note prayers from the students involved in this week's morning services. The room provides a space, like many school chapels, for quiet reflection, but it is also the central hub for a network of students seeking to 'make a difference'.

Sitting there one day last November my early morning cup of tea was interrupted by two sixth-formers fetching posters and collection boxes, explaining how they were supporting a group of Year 9 fundraisers at lunchtime. As the bell rang, the room then became a worship space and the chaplain led daily morning worship for one vertical form.[3] The students were given the opportunity to write prayers on post-it notes (some were personal, but the plight of the Syrian refugees was a concern for many). As the bell for break rang, the form group dispersed and a mixed-age group of student volunteers entered to discuss organising next week's Children in Need[4] Day. At lunchtime, the room hosted a large enthusiastic group of Year 9 students for 'cell group' (a Christian meeting) led by Year 11 students and sixth-formers. At the end of the day, the chaplaincy room was filled again with students for a meeting of the Global Justice group. Others came to collect materials for a Fairtrade event or to clarify arrangements for meeting at the local mosque for a Leeds Citizens event. Later on that evening a small group of parents would come to that same room to pray for the academy community. This glimpse into chaplaincy highlights two key aspects of spiritual development in Abbey Grange Academy – student involvement in social action and student leadership in Christian witness.

Faith in action

> I like to help people when nobody else can and I know that I can't save the world but I can try and help with some of the bigger issues. (Student)

When I asked students in Abbey Grange Academy about spiritual development they told me about the social action they were involved in and the opportunities that the academy had given them to develop skills to enable them to be 'the change they want to see'. Young people are often full of enthusiasm to change the world; what became apparent in conversations with students in Abbey Grange was that many believed that they could make a difference. They gave examples of when they had made a difference, raising money for a wide variety of charities, raising awareness of issues of local and global justice, supporting other students in the academy and actively volunteering in the local community. Why did so many students in this academy want to make a difference to their community? The key to understanding this was to be found in a view of Christianity as a faith of action, in an academy that prioritised empowering students to become leaders not of the future, but of the here and now.

To give just one example: Makkah Mosque in Leeds is a beautiful purpose-built mosque (2003); in February 2015 it hosted one of the first meetings of the newly formed Leeds Citizens group. The mosque was crowded. I sat with the academy chaplain and a small group of Abbey Grange students. Representatives of many different communities from across Leeds came together to explore how they could make a difference within the city. The purpose of the evening was to select a

> For me, as a human being, I feel I have a moral obligation to try and give something to the community and try and put my mark on trying to stop some of the poverty and severe injustice that takes place. (Student)

> Sometimes people don't know that they want to make a difference until they're shown that you can really make a difference. (Student)

small number of achievable projects. An Abbey Grange student stood in front of the crowded room to explain why she and her fellow students wanted to be part of this movement for positive change in the city of Leeds. The students came away buzzing, already planning the next meeting, which they had offered to host at Abbey Grange Academy. As hosts of the next meeting, with Michael* (Year 11) as co-chair and Rachel* (Year 11) as secretary, they listened carefully to all views, made sure that all remained focused, and helped develop a clear plan of action. Catching up with them a few months later, they proudly explained the differences that they had made to bus transport in Leeds and described how they were now recruiting, developing and supporting other younger students to become involved.

> **The influence of the focus on faith in action is apparent in the Year 9 and 10 students' responses to the two statements below:**
>
> 76% – I would like to make a difference in the world
>
> 77% – I am concerned about the poverty of the developing world (e.g. Africa)

The Archbishop of York Young Leaders Award

The YLA embodies the principles of '*educere*', and provides genuine opportunities for young people to grow in faith, leadership, character, and service. Within each award every young person takes part in a social action project for the benefit of the community.
(Archbishop John Sentamu)

Underpinning this hub of social action in Abbey Grange Academy was the Archbishop of York Young Leaders Award (AYYLA)[5]. The Archbishop of York Youth Trusts has worked with over 400 primary and secondary schools, empowering some 46,000 young people to make a difference in their communities.[6] The Award consists of three modules in Key Stage 3 and ten in Key Stage 4. It introduces students to Christians who have put their faith into action and aims to develop 'soft skills' such as public speaking, campaigning and organising charity events, within the context of Christian social action.

In the Abbey Grange Academy, the AYYLA modules were embedded within the curriculum and mapped onto and integrated with the existing programme of faith and social action in the academy. Students were enthusiastic about involvement in the AYYLA; it was very different from other lessons. In March 2015 a small low-ability Year 9 class were learning about public speaking: they had to speak for five minutes before the whole class, a daunting task. When I met up with them again in October, Hannah* told me how despite her initial feelings of trepidation this experience had increased her confidence in and outside the academy.

[AYYLA] is teaching you that you can change the world with your actions if you put faith before everything.
(Student)

It's quite an adult thing to do because you're not treated like children. It's teaching you to stand up for something that you know is right.
(Student)

In October 2015, a different Year 9 class were evaluating their latest task to raise awareness of World Food Day. One group of four students had, on their own initiative, taken their presentation into the local primary school on the Friday before, when they were not in school as it had been a teachers' in-service day in Abbey Grange Academy. Other students in the class had designed, printed, laminated and put up posters around the academy to raise awareness of food waste.

When Year 11 students reflected on their five years of working towards the AYYLA, they highlighted how the experience had:

- shown me how I could help others, for example, to speak in front of other people;

- helped me to develop skills that were now put to use in campaigning for the homeless;

- taught me skills that now enabled my active leadership role in the Leeds section of Citizens UK;

- made me keen to raise awareness that it was not just about passing the award, but that you can make a difference.

Senior leadership had made the deliberate decision to embed the AYYLA into the whole curriculum, enabling all students to develop the skills and to develop an awareness of their Christian faith as a faith of social action. The principal stressed how AYYLA was not an add-on: it encompassed the academy ethos, fitted with the mission statement and contributed to the spiritual and moral development of all students. The chaplain's role was crucial. Sustaining the role of a chaplain (four days per week) and being passionate about empowering students was essential to facilitating the opportunities for students. Enabling student-led involvement in the academic community, in the local community and in national and international campaigns takes time. The initial up-skilling of students, liaising with outside agencies, does in the long term empower more students to be involved and take leadership roles and enables more social action to happen, but the initial time commitment should not be underestimated.

Empowered to love, care and serve

I continue to be amazed by the things I see and hear when young people are empowered to love, care and serve their communities with passion and dedication. (Archbishop John Sentamu)[7]

We need to develop strategies to help children transform themselves into positive change agents and begin creating a new model which empowers young people to make a difference.[8]

Often within Christian education the emphasis on spiritual development falls on developing students' beliefs and attitudes and encouraging them to experience Christian worship practices. Rarely is the spotlight shone on the application of Christian social teaching not as a classroom study but in practice. For some staff and students an emphasis on empowering students enables the development of essential soft skills. However, the emphasis on social action, seeing action for justice as a priority, is in this Church of England academy viewed in the context of Christian teachings and scriptures. Indeed, as Dan Finn, Director of the Archbishop of York Youth Trust, explains, students are given the opportunity not only to grasp the meaning of the parable of the sheep and the goats, but to seek ways to apply it within their school community, their local community and wider.

This approach to spiritual development adopts the view that human beings made in the image of God are called to serve each other. An influence on this approach is an understanding that Christianity is underpinned by a call for social justice. The implications for Christian education are, in the words of Archbishop John Sentamu, a need for a refocus on *educere*, 'education that draws out that which lies within', and a need to provide young people with opportunities to put their beliefs into action.

Therefore, the role of Christian education should be to empower young people to make a difference to their community and the wider world. This can be done by adopting a framework like the AYYLA that enables young people to develop the skills needed, and provides them with opportunities to make a difference.

> **Not only does God call us to live life abundantly as individuals made in his image and likeness, he calls us to serve one another in community – living and flourishing together.**
> (Archbishop John Sentamu)[9]

Empowering students as Christian leaders

> **Does the Bible mention the second ice age?**
>
> **How did people live so long in Noah's time?**
>
> **Did God place the sheep on the mountain for Abraham to sacrifice instead of Isaac?**
> (Student)

Did Noah take dinosaurs on board the ark? This question was put to the student leaders of a Year 10 cell group (a voluntary meeting of students interested in developing knowledge and sharing Christian faith) one lunchtime in October 2015. In the chaplaincy room were a group of Year 10 boys and three student leaders, Andrew* and Jonathan* (sixth-formers) and Rebekah* (Year 11).

Rebekah had prepared the material for this session, which fitted into this term's theme of reading the Old Testament through the lens of the New Testament. The questions from the Year 10 boys flowed thick and fast during the lively discussion. The student leaders drew on their own faith and their study of the Bible in giving their responses; Jonathan introduced the symbolism that linked these stories in Genesis with the life of Jesus. The session, which had begun so noisily with much chatter and the eating of lunch, concluded with prayers for personal concerns, school issues, and thanks for the meeting and for my work in the academy.

These cell group meetings were highlighted by several students as the major influence on their spiritual development in this academy. The students encouraged me to visit their cell group. It was a place to come together, where you could 'feel like a family' and 'connect with God in different ways'. It was essential that people came, as what happened in cell was 'really important'. All the students stressed the sense of belonging to a small group and the influence of the student leadership. The student leaders were respected and seen as more approachable than adult leaders.

The cell group format had existed in Abbey Grange for about 12 years. In practice it meant that Year 7 had a lively activity-based meeting focused on a Bible topic led by Leeds Faith in Schools.[10] Years 8, 9 and 10 had a lunchtime meeting in the chaplaincy room, led by older students, which involved time for the eating of lunch, icebreaker games and a Bible or prayer-focused activity. Years 11–13 had a lunchtime session involving more focused Bible study or a prayer session. It was facilitated and resourced by the chaplain, who liaised with external agencies, such as Leeds Faith in Schools, and also by Missional Generation.[11]

The Missional Generation charity was keen to support the work in Abbey Grange Academy as it fitted with their aims to help young people become 'influential for God'. The cell group model was about connection and community – a place of safety and a place of questioning. The training of the peer leaders was crucial; it included showing the students that learning can be fun and how to create an inclusive environment with faith at the centre of it.

An extract from an interview with Andrew* (Year 13), a leader of the Year 10 cell group

The guy who got me involved used to get my bus, it's really bizarre. Because I used to sit with him on the bus and we got talking about faith. I had no particular views … it got me interested and I started asking a lot of questions. He was like, you're asking me so much questions – here, have a Bible. So he gave me my first Bible.

The role models in school [are important] because a lot of other people are good examples of model Christians … you can become like that if you try hard enough. [My role model is] probably one of the guys who runs cell, Andrew*. He's a pretty chilled guy. (J. Year 10)

I read the Bible outside of school as well. Like you read it in cell, the sixth-formers find a quote in the Bible, bring it to cell and then we all read it and we interpret from it. Normally we all have different answers, which is good. (M. Year 10)

There's one particular book in the Old Testament actually, Joshua. That's my favourite book and it's the book that made me a Christian. It's in chapter 1, verses 6–9, that says – this is paraphrasing – be strong and courageous and I think it's God motivating. It just really spoke to me and it made me feel like, wow, God is this really empowering being. It's absolutely amazing.

It's about showing them the way. You can't force someone to do something; it's about letting them find their own feet and showing them the right path and them choosing to go towards that themselves. The Year 10s are getting to that stage where they could be potential leaders. Because I've been with them for a year I do see which ones could be leader. It's just a matter of maturity and respect sometimes. They may be Year 10s but sometimes they come out like Year 7s and I do love the fun and games we all have, but sometimes it's just hard to get them focused.

The people who run the cell group, they can give you options of how to bring up your own faith. They discuss it with you so you can discuss it and you can talk about it. (E. Year 10)

My attitude to life is more positive and more respectful ... that's probably down to me being a Christian ... because I've been going to cell since Year 7 and it's just like made me mature, if that makes sense. (J. Year 10)

The cell groups and cell leaders keep me going through the week knowing that there's still people who want to get to know God. I try not to think of myself as a leader because I am equally growing in my faith as they are. I'm guiding the topic by saying we're going to talk about this. But then I am no better to talk about it than they are, they equally can talk about it. So it's good to always have that in mind, that you're no better than anyone else, you can only learn.

I always think things would have been so much more different for me personally because it's here that I became Christian. It's the people who came here that moulded my faith and I just always wonder what would have happened if I'd gone to another school that maybe wasn't as encouraging with faith. I may never have found it. So I'm very grateful for all the things that go on here.

Students as Christian role models

[The aim] is to help young people to become influential for God.
(Ben Jones, Missional Generation)

Empowering students to become Christian role models, to lead Christian cell groups within a school, has many challenges. These include, for example, the fact that the student leaders, like all leaders, are themselves in the process of developing, of thinking through, their faith. In Abbey Grange Academy these challenges are addressed through a close collaboration between the chaplain and external Christian agencies such as Missional Generation and Leeds Faith in Schools. A key element is supporting the young leaders by listening to their questions and doubts and providing opportunities for further development, such as the academy's annual retreat and opportunities outside school with local churches and Christian charities. The relationship between academy and external agencies is crucial. The aims and purposes of the latter must be compatible with the ethos of this academy.

The influence of Christian youth ministry approaches is apparent in the cell group format, and many of these young leaders are active in church youth groups. The student-led cell group model in Abbey Grange has addressed an issue raised in many of the Ten Leading Schools, namely that of the young Christian who is active in his/her church community but is not involved in any explicitly Christian activities in school. A reason often put forward by staff and chaplains is that these students have the perception that they are 'getting their fix' of Christianity elsewhere and have no need of what is offered in school. The model at Abbey Grange Academy, which empowers students to be leaders, offers these students opportunities to understand what they as young Christian role models can offer to other students within the academy.

Chapter overview

- Faith in action
- Archbishop of York Young Leaders Award
- Empowered to love, care and serve
- Empowering students as Christian leaders
- Students as Christian role models

Endnotes

* pseudonym

1. Fairtrade Yorkshire: http://www.fairtradeyorkshire.org.uk/category/schools

2. Leeds Citizens: http://www.citizensuk.org/leeds

3. The vertical form system means that each form includes students from across the school Years 7–11.

4. Children in Need Day: annual fundraising day for the BBC's UK charity.

5. See Archbishop of York Youth Trust website: http://www.archbishopofyorkyouthtrust.co.uk/

6. Figures accurate as of December 2016 – email from Director of Archbishop of York Trust.

7. See http://www.archbishopofyorkyouthtrust.co.uk/news/2016/05/19/nurturing-heart-mind-and-soul-spiritual-context-education-archbishop-york/

8. Boggs, Grace Lee (2009), 'Youth and Social Justice in Education'. In W. Ayers, T. Quinn and D. Stovall (eds), Handbook of Social Justice in Education. New York: Routledge.

9. Sentamu, John, Archbishop of York (2016), 'Nurturing the Heart, Mind and Soul: The Spiritual Context of Education'. *Schools for Human Flourishing.* London: National Society Church of England https://www.churchofengland.org/media/2492341/schools_for_human_flourishing.pdf

10. Leeds Faith in Schools: http://www.lfis.org/

11. Missional Generation: https://www.missionalgen.co.uk/

3

Prioritising hope

Key ideas: hope; values education; social justice

Students in St Mary Redcliffe and Temple School said:

63% God is very real to me

64% I know that Jesus helps me

66% I believe that God listens to prayers

47% I am a spiritual person

65% I am a religious person

ST MARY REDCLIFFE AND TEMPLE SCHOOL (CHURCH OF ENGLAND), BRISTOL

Coeducational comprehensive school

11–18 years

c.1,700 students

The glory of God is the human being fully alive.

St Mary Redcliffe and Temple School (SMRT), Bristol is a long-established city-centre Church of England school in which students and staff identified myriad features that contributed to their spiritual development. The concept that connected these many features was hope: hope understood in terms of the Christian faith as a confident expectation based on trust in God.

In SMRT, a quiet observer of the daily life of the school quickly gains a sense of a Christian ethos centred on hope:

- Listening to a teacher explain that he became a teacher to give hope to those who 'don't have much hope'.

- Reflecting with a senior leader on the theme for the 2015 improvement plan; 'we are all imperfect people in a climate of hope'.

- Encountering stories about a cow named Hope in Ikoba secondary school, Uganda, named in honour of a school partnership that is based on 'hope because that's at the centre of our school'.

The stories of hope told within SMRT are framed by a well-established model of learning, the Alive model, based on Christian values and rooted in Irenaeus' understanding that the glory of God is a human being fully alive. The Alive model, developed within SMRT, is a structured integrated model of values, which permeates the whole of the school ethos, teaching and learning, pastoral care and worship. I have adopted this model as a lens to view the story of spiritual development here, selecting just four of these values: justice, forgiveness, trust and faith.

The glory of God is the human person fully alive. (Bishop Irenaeus of Lyons)

> **It is intangible, something about diversity, where everyone is valued.**
> (Parent)

A group of parents, waiting to see teachers at a Year 10 parents' evening, shared their views of the 'uniqueness' of this school. Their conclusion was that the essence is the values that run through SMRT and underpin everything that happens; children were valued as individuals, with God-given gifts.

The Alive model includes 15 values, skills and competencies firmly rooted in the Christian foundation of the school community:

- I value: faith, myself, trust and truth, forgiveness, justice and respect.

- I am: creative, resilient, organised, questioning, interdependent.

- I can: plan, revise, review, research, communicate.

> **The Alive theme, that's to do with things that you should practise during the week. [For example] one statement could be 'I could be resilient.'**
> (Student)

It was developed in response to two main questions:

- What is it to be fully human?

- What environment enables that to happen?

> **Spiritual development within this school is very much centred on the Alive model. We want to see every young person understand that they are valued and precious and that they have a place in this school community and in the wider community of the city and beyond.** (Staff)

The 15 values are embedded in the curriculum and in the collective worship programme. Induction into the nature of the Alive model is integral to the development of all staff and students. Exploring student and staff engagement with four of the values – justice, forgiveness, trust and faith – offers a glimpse of the variety of ways in which the Alive model centred on hope contributes to spiritual development in all areas of school life.

I value justice

A value that resonated throughout my many encounters in SMRT, reflecting that sense of hope and the value of giving hope to others, was justice. In SMRT 'I value justice' involves putting 'your whole self into action and exploration' (head teacher) and 'an engagement with learning and the world outside school' (stakeholder).

I value justice and respect: I can identify situations within – and beyond – my own experience which are unjust and I do whatever is within my power to set them right, while showing that I am able to accept other people's understanding of these situations. (Alive model of learning – SMRT)

The head teacher draws a clear connection between justice and spiritual development. She argues that in young people a sense of spirituality is closely connected with a sense of justice and a desire to act, to do something to make a difference. The school then has a role to provide opportunities to give students 'an outlet' to actually change the world for the better. Enabling students to engage with social justice issues in their school, local community and the wider community emphasises that human beings cannot flourish without others flourishing in their communities. To put it in the language and concepts of SMRT, this means that being 'fully alive' oneself is inextricably linked to bringing hope to others to enable them to be fully alive.

The sixth form in SMRT has a strong emphasis on issues of social justice and inclusion, with a focus on developing young people not only as 'whole people but as citizens' (staff). Sixth-formers spoke of the work they were involved in, defending human rights across the city of Bristol. For example, one group of sixth-form students wanted to raise awareness of rape and sexual abuse and had created a workshop to show in assemblies and to take out to other schools in Bristol. Some students argued that their involvement in this work was motivated by their Christian faith; others stressed it was a duty of all humans, no matter what their religious background.

The content of lessons like music lends itself to the expression of such values as justice. The creative arts in general were an area that students and staff highlighted as providing opportunities to reflect on the Alive values. The music teacher gave the example of studying blues music – that is, 'an expression by a certain people at a certain time' where the clashing discordant notes demonstrate that 'we don't quite fit, don't quite belong here' and which always raises questions around issues of justice.

[Values education] comes out strongly in music. You have to be brave if you're going to create a piece of music from scratch and so you have to value yourself therefore. As soon as it's been performed you have to value others because you are listening to what someone else has created. (Staff)

I've always known that around the world there's so much injustice and I think there's a song that says we must go to feed the hungry, stand beside the broken. I always thought that song is so true. Our mission should be to help others. It's so important to me, in terms of human rights. People should have those rights everywhere. (Student)

I'm proud to be part of a sixth form that's renowned for its social impact and its attention to social justice. (Student)

> **The partnership between Ikoba secondary school and SMRT developed the spirit of love in my life.**
> (Email from Mukonyezi Hope Doreen, Ikoba)

One fruitful result of this focus on issues of social justice and bringing hope to others is the partnership between SMRT and Ikoba, a secondary school in rural Uganda. This influences the spiritual development of staff and students in both schools and flourishes in the climate of hope engendered in SMRT and in the opportunities created to bring hope to communities outside of school.

The basis of the relationship between the two schools has always been one of a partnership, one in which the whole school community is involved. The teacher in charge, recognising that only a few would be able to visit Ikoba itself, put strategies in place to ensure that this relationship would involve all students.

> **In Africa there are broken promises. We wanted to restore some of the broken promises which other people had made. Ikoba had been promised a cow which never arrived, so we raised money for the cow, which they called Hope. It was a milker cow, which is quite expensive, but it now has a calf called Peace!** (Staff)

The partnership is very visible in school: in assemblies; in the school prayer in the student planner, which is 'basically the same as the Ikoba school prayer'; in the active 'pen pal' relationship between the students of the two schools; and in the exchange visits between students and staff from SMRT and staff and students from Ikoba.

> **We just tell them about what is going on in our lives and what is going on in the school and things like that and they reply ... they're a Christian school as well so we pray for each other as well.**
> (Student)

Each year all of the Year 7 students are involved in Ikoba Partnership Day, which always begins with a Eucharist. In 2015 this opened with a video of Ikoba students singing the first hymn, and followed the Kenyan rite. The sermon focused on needing to understand how others see things. Throughout the day students were involved in various lessons and activities, some of which were led by staff and students who have visited Ikoba.

> **The partnership they do and try and immerse you through school but it's very different being there and seeing things. Being there you sort of feel a very personal connection all of a sudden because they're so overjoyed to have you there and it's just it feels like they all know you already, which is very strange.**
> (Student)

Fundraising for Ikoba goes on throughout the year. In 2015 Year 7 students raised money that provided the equivalent of free school meals for the 'day students' in Ikoba. The sixth form have had a couple of 'rag weeks' where Ikoba has been one of the main charities, and from those weeks equipped the Ikoba sixth form with books and materials.

Some of the older students who had visited Ikoba highlighted that they had been impressed with the hospitality, faith and the sense of hope in the Ikoba school. The sense of engaging with the reality of issues of social justice and giving hope to others was made visible in the partnership developed between these two school communities.

I value forgiveness

I value forgiveness: Forgiveness involves taking responsibility for putting things right and giving someone the opportunity to start again. (Alive model of learning – SMRT)

'Imperfect people in a climate of hope' was the title of the school improvement plan for 2015. As one member of staff explained, this was in recognition that 'we are all human beings and will all mess up'. The aim was that through exploring this theme this year, it would enable a 'particular focus on forgiveness'.

One morning in 2015, a group of Year 7 students were tasked with reviewing an assembly on forgiveness delivered by their peers. The four students had put great efforts into their assembly, including several Bible quotes (Ephesians 4.32; Acts 7.59–60), a video clip of an interview with a murder victim's mother, and a role play of the story of the prodigal son, and had also written their own poems and prayers. The young reviewers complimented the planning and organisation and offered constructive criticism on delivery and timings. They then considered the relevance of the theme of forgiveness for their year group. The students reflected how appropriate the message of this assembly, that 'we must forgive as God forgives us', had been at a time in their school lives when they were meeting with many new people, who inevitably did not always 'get along' and 'forgot to say sorry to each other'.

The theme of forgiveness was echoed by older students involved in the school drama production of *Les Misérables*. The drama teacher reflected on the centrality of God and forgiveness to the musical and how they encouraged the students to reflect and to question the faith of the characters.

The climate of hope is the fact that we believe that God has everything in control and is greater than human ability, even at times when it's difficult to see that, and the valuing of each other when things go wrong, whether we're students or staff. (Staff)

If you think something is wrong you should question it, that's something I try to instil. *Les Mis* gave you that inlet because you were able to put it into a context of something that they were enjoying doing, based in faith. (Staff)

I was watching *Songs of Praise* one day and one of our ex-students was on there. He said that one of the things that had helped him in his life all the way through is this RE lesson on the ups and downs of Joseph's life. It does make you think sometimes, doesn't it, of the impact of what goes on. (Staff)

I value trust

The value of trust centred in the concept of hope was apparent in a Year 8 Religious Education (RE) lesson. Students had been given a task to evaluate whether the biblical character of Joseph had applied or not applied the Alive values in his lifetime. The students were confident in identifying the values Joseph had applied, such as faith, trust and forgiveness; Joseph had 'trusted in God' even though God had tested him. They also pointed out the many times when Joseph might have 'done better' if he had applied more of the Alive values.

One morning the value of trust was the theme for Chris* during another Year 8 student's tutor worship. He delivered an action-packed worship for his tutor group (in SMRT main school, Years 8–11, tutor groups are 'vertical' and include students from all four years). The assembly began with the Martin Luther King quote, 'Faith is taking the first step without seeing the whole staircase', provided examples from the Gospels (the wedding at Cana and Jesus walking on water; and then, before the concluding prayer, included a video clip of 'the leap of faith' from *Indiana Jones and the Last Crusade*. After the worship finished, Chris confidently explained to me why he had chosen each example and how it linked to the Alive theme of trust, of trusting in God.

I value faith

One of the fundamental values of the Alive model is the value of faith. Again, it is the understanding of faith as a reflection of Christian hope in God. The value is framed in an inclusive manner, reminding students that it is important not only to be able to recognise and understand their faith and the faith of others, but also to be able to articulate their own beliefs if they do not have a religious faith or are not sure.

The value of faith was identified and expressed by students in a variety of ways: in the enthusiasm of the chaplain in chaplaincy activities at lunchtime, in prayer and in worship in school. For example, a group of Year 11 students talked me through the Eucharist that they had recently organised and led. Their aim had been to have a 'real' service, to try and 'connect with God' like you would in a church and to 'speak with students on a deeper level'. They had planned to do this by sharing their lives, experiences and their faith. In the Eucharist itself some of the students had spoken about their faith story.

The students reflected on the impact that 'their' Eucharist had had on their peers and on themselves. They shared examples where students had come up to them and said, 'I'm inspired', which motivated them to be more involved in organising worship.

A space for faith is offered in the two chaplaincy rooms: room 91 (inspired by Psalm 91) and room 42 (42 is the answer given to the question about the meaning of life in Douglas Adams' book *The Hitchhiker's Guide to the Galaxy*). Spending time with students, staff and chaplain here gave an insight into how many students in SMRT not only valued faith but were passionate about sharing it with their peers.

The openness to faith is fantastic, and I love being around people who are as passionate about God as I am. I can't tell you how much I love running Christian Union. Seeing God move and answer our prayers in school is so exciting, and has really developed my faith, and I am developing loads of skills in leadership and ministry and planning. (Student, Christian Union leader)

I was talking about how I give God thanks for [getting into the team], I was grateful for that. People asked me why I don't do things like swear and I thought that if God helped me get into [the team] then I should pay him back in a way and tell people that I don't swear because I'm a Christian and start telling them about my faith. (Student)

You can never know the full impact because obviously we can't see [the students'] relationship with God after that. But students have come up to us and said thank you for the assembly, it has changed their view of their faith. (Student)

Room 42 is a total blessing. Our main aim is to provide a warm and welcoming space where people feel able to come and talk about their views and share ideas and be accepted whatever their beliefs. We have a big emphasis on outreach. (Student)

This passion was apparent when the sixth-form students spoke of their leadership of and involvement with the Christian Union. The students' approach to leadership was influenced by the chaplain's modelling of faith leadership; his emphasis on being a presence; praying; and developing partnerships.

A climate of hope

These stories told in SMRT focus around a sense of Christian hope, the sense of bringing hope to others – hope in the form of God's forgiveness, hope found in trust, and the sharing of one's faith. Encountering and engaging with the concept of hope expressed in these values, through the Alive model, creates an environment in which spiritual development can take place.

> **At the centre of the school development plan is hope, and circled around hope are the key elements needed to create this positive environment.**
> (Staff)

The question to be asked is, how does a school create such an environment, a 'climate of hope'? One factor within SMRT is the development of the Alive model, an effective model of values that is 'owned' by students and staff. Maintaining this model so it is relevant to each new intake of staff and students is essential. In SMRT a clear process could be identified to ensure its relevance to each new generation. The process involved a clear focus on the fundamental aims; an emphasis on inclusivity; an integration of the model into all aspects of school life; and constant review and reinterpretation when necessary.

It is important that the key aims for the school environment, those of 'safe boundaries, good relationships, empowered learning', remain constant. These aims are 'all held together in that sense of Christian hope' (head teacher). To facilitate these aims in a school setting, a school needs to create 'a climate of hope'. Creating such an environment requires detailed forethought; it is about creating a safe space, where relationships can develop built on trust, and where young people can become 'active and interdependent reflective learners'. It is a holistic view of the person, where spiritual development and academic development go together.

> **Our development plan is always based on what we believe young people need to grow and flourish and become fully alive. That has been our journey, that is our present and that is our future. There's a solidity and a consistency to that.**
> (Head teacher)

The inclusive nature of the Alive model is important. The idea of becoming 'fully alive' is seen as accessible to people of all faiths and none – 'you don't need to be a Christian to think what it means to be fully alive' (head teacher). It assumes an understanding of all human beings as having a spiritual dimension. Becoming 'fully alive' is to develop spiritually, and each individual becomes 'fully alive' in their own unique way.

> **Spiritual development [is] becoming the person that God intended you to be. You are formed in the womb and known by God that formed us; that is the ultimate sense of what our spiritual journey is, it's about becoming fully human, fully alive.**
> (Stakeholder)

A strength of this model is integrated into all aspects of school life – the curriculum, collective worship, pastoral care and professional development. This integration ensures that it informs the language of students and staff and shapes the way in which teaching and learning is understood. It reflects a understanding that spiritual development needs an holistic approach to be effective; it is not confined to RE, collective worship or the role of the chaplain.

The final essential factor in the effectiveness of SMRT's Alive values model of education is that it is not 'set in stone', but is constantly reviewed and reinterpreted for each new generation of students and staff. Senior leadership reflect on the needs of each academic year to inform the priorities of the school development plan and prioritise accordingly. The strengths of this approach are that it is not locked down – it is creative and open to interpretation. This successfully works in SMRT because it is adapted to the needs of this specific school community. It builds on the strengths of members of that community, and on the nature of the Christian ethos generated by the mix of students and staff.

Chapter overview

- 'The glory of God is the human person fully alive.'
- I value justice
- I value forgiveness
- I value trust
- I value faith
- A climate of hope

Endnote

* pseudonym

4

An inclusive community

Key ideas: community; collective worship; inclusivity

BISHOP JUSTUS CHURCH OF ENGLAND SCHOOL, BROMLEY

Coeducational comprehensive school

11–18 years

c.1,400 students

Motto: Through faith and learning

Where in a school do you look for the features that positively contribute to spiritual development? You could spend some time, as I did, in the school chapel at Bishop Justus Church of England School and encounter an Anglican morning prayer session, a lunchtime Eucharist, and a thought-provoking discussion about African religion with a local youth pastor.

You could investigate morning worship, wander into an assembly in the main hall or sit quietly in form worship listening to animated discussions followed by quiet reflection. You could spend time in RE lessons listening to animated student-led discussions on a wide variety of religious and moral issues. In my time doing just that in Bishop Justus School I became aware of students and staff actively engaged in thinking and reflecting on the spiritual dimension of life.

However, it is often the less visible, the less quantifiable, that students and staff in Bishop Justus identified as positively influencing their spiritual development. It was the hello in the corridor; 'just the people'; the principal 'knowing your name'; the kindness of the catering staff when you were suffering and when you were celebrating. It was a sense that this school is welcoming to all. It was the tea and cakes in the staff room once a week, or the chocolate bars for all staff just because everyone was stressed with marking. It was in quiet moments of reflection, the prayers shared with others daily and at times of crisis. It was not just in the school chapel or classrooms but in the music practice rooms, or the changing rooms before a big game. It was knowing that in the corridors and the school yard, in conversations at break, or lunchtime with friends, you could talk about your faith. The Christian ethos of this school was embedded in the 'hidden things'; it was underpinned with a strong sense of belonging to a Christian community.

In April 2004, the newly appointed principal of the Bishop Justus School was faced with a daunting task: how do you start a Church of England secondary school from scratch? Fast forward ten years and Bishop Justus is a school community with 'a connection to God' [student] where 'spirituality is everywhere' [staff]. A school community that believes itself 'quite different' from any other school – and the key to that difference is 'because we're very inclusive, God's at the heart of our community' [principal].

I stood in the field in wellies with an architect's drawing and said, I'll have our school here . . . there was nothing, not even a paper clip. We had to build a school community from scratch. The first thing was laying those firm foundations. From the outset, we were outstanding in terms of [the Christian ethos], knowing that if you get that right everything else is going to follow, but you've got to get that right, [and] protect it fiercely. (Principal)

This place gives you a sense of belonging. This place is a community; I take it for granted until I talk about it. This place is an absolute community that I'm very lucky to be in and a lot of people's professional lives will never feel that. (Staff)

The head teacher characterised the sense of community as a sense of togetherness in a school community. A community where 'all individuals being completely different from each other share a sense of belonging to this one place where we can all get along' results in a togetherness. This concept of 'togetherness' encompasses a sense of inclusion; it emphasises diversity and stresses that individuality is not 'merely' tolerated, but celebrated.

The intriguing question is how Bishop Justus School had developed from 'not even a paper clip' to an inclusive community with God at its centre, a school community influencing the spiritual development of all within it. What is there about the nature of this school community? In fact, many factors and many people contributed to this sense of belonging, as will be seen as the story unfolds in this chapter.

Morning worship – making 'connections'

[Worship is] just like the main thing that makes a Christian
school Christian…without worship or talking to God, [Bishop Justus]
wouldn't be a Christian school. (Student)

For many students, the daily worship with their form class contributed to their spiritual development; it was where they talked about and reflected on spiritual matters. It provided a space to question, challenge and reflect.

Our daily worship is really important. They're quite creative in the way they make you interact with them. That's good because it stimulates thought and religious perspectives, allowing you to develop spiritually without forcing it on individuals who don't necessarily associate themselves with that. (Student)

The key element of the worship was, in the words of the principal, the opportunity for 'distinctively Christian reflection': real reflection, a time to develop deeper feelings, to think about how 'God might be speaking to you'. It was an open and inclusive time, a challenge to all to reflect on the worship theme.

You feel like you want to connect with God. (Student)

My form tutor gives us a few moments before the prayer just to reflect on the whole worship, and I think that allows Christians and non-Christians to think about the worship. (Student)

A prime example of this could be found in morning worship in the Learning Access area. This was a space where small group interventions took place (such as English as an additional language, extra literacy and numeracy, critical thinking, speech and language and social skills). The SENCo first drew my attention to the practice of morning worship with these learners. For him it summed up what Bishop Justus was all about.

The aim is that we take the PowerPoints, and the message, in advance. We then adapt it, so for example literacy, the stories that are given from the Bible or a parable or whatever, are then broken down and talked through, all about the meaning… then that's done for a specific amount of time and then any specific literacy-based activities are done afterwards as well. (Staff)

[This] is safe sanctuary…a core group of 'anxious' learners come in every morning for safety, security and peace of mind. (Staff)

> **God sort of is there to help you along with your learning.**
> (Student)

One day in January 2016, the teaching assistant was supporting Year 10 students with extra English. It was a mixed group. The majority were 'regulars' and had been meeting together in this place once a week since Year 7. This day the worship was student-led by Ed*, who had prepared the material for discussion, made sure all took part, and listened 'respectfully'.

This worship focused on Moses' appeal to Pharaoh. Led by Ed, the students had a lively discussion on the role of government in biblical times and in their own lives, followed by quiet reflection on how that Bible passage could be relevant in their lives, today. The students described worship as a time that was 'basically private', with a group of their peers they knew well, with whom they had an opportunity to explore a 'connection to God'.

> **[Morning worship] is about having an out of and in-school connection to God obviously. For others who 'don't believe in God or Christianity, they still get some sort of message out of it, because it still projects out goodness into them'.** (Ed*)

> **I have grown up doing [worship] in a 'religious' family; it makes good sense to bring religion into learning.**
> (Student)

For these students who may not find their voice elsewhere, within this small group they had established a worshipping community. The security of being in a safe place meant, as one student explained, that there was 'more faith between each other'. The staff explained that because 'our learners sometimes aren't as articulate, don't have the social skills, the small groups really allow them to have a voice'. This morning worship in a place and time where they felt safe provided an opportunity to develop spiritual awareness.

This sense of a worshipping community was enabled by the deliberate decision of the senior leadership to prioritise morning worship, together with an emphasis on ensuring it was accessible to all. The senior leadership had made a clear decision that morning worship should be prioritised. As a consequence, form time had been extended and 20 minutes every morning was protected worship time. It was monitored through staff and student reviews and the expectation that worship occurred every morning was accepted as the norm.

Delivering meaningful collective worship in a church school with a diverse student intake is both a challenge and an opportunity. A barrier to full engagement in collective worship is an inability to fully understand the liturgy, the scriptural references, the religious terminology employed. An awareness and understanding of the students' diverse levels of general, religious and theological literacy should inevitably influence the content and format of worship. Collective worship offers an opportunity to develop these aspects of literacy and enable all students and staff to fully engage in meaningful worship.

In the Bishop Justus School the worship resources had been carefully thought through to ensure that they were inclusive, recognising the different needs of individual students. In an action research project undertaken by the head of literacy, some Year 8 students had identified some barriers to accessing worship. The discussions in worship did not always allow time for all students to reflect and process the questions asked and students did not fully understand some of the key words used. There was thus a need to explain these religious/theological terms in context. This approach is dependent on tutors understanding the religious and theological terms, so within Bishop Justus active support for teachers is provided by the chaplain and other key members of staff.

Accessible worship:

- Slow it down.

- Put the key questions up so they can see the question before it's discussed so they can read it, and process it.

- Give time to discuss it with each other, before students' feedback.

- Pick up on key words and explain them and put them into the context of their own lives, so that they understand how things interrelate to each other. (Staff)

One of the things that [the students] highlighted is that [worship] makes them part of the community ... it doesn't matter what faith you are, you can still get involved in discussing things ... and they like the sense that they know everybody is doing this, everybody is part of this. (Staff)

In the story of the Bishop Justus School it could be seen that collective worship is a major contributor both to the Christian ethos and to the spiritual development of its students. This sense of community, of belonging to a Christian community, was strengthened by the prioritising of daily worship.

Faith conversations

One consequence of this strong sense of community is that it provided an environment, a safe space, where students could explore and discuss their spiritual identity and talk about spiritual matters. For example, I met with John* three times over the course of two years of research. He was an articulate, thoughtful Year 10 student who was keen to explain why his time in this school had had such an effect on his Christian faith. He sought to describe the key element and he came to the conclusion that it was 'the people here', with whom he felt comfortable to discuss his faith.

There are quite a lot of opportunities to talk to people about Christ and they're quite open to it. Often having a school friend who shows you what it's really like to be a Christian – I think that helps a lot. Outside the classroom, sometimes at break and lunch, it sounds really boring, but we start talking about faith.
(Student)

An openness to talking about faith was shared by many students from other faith or non-religious backgrounds. In the survey of Year 9 and 10 students in 2015, two-thirds thought that their friends thought that religion was important. Talking about faith was viewed as important for spiritual development. It was seen as essential to have 'people you can talk to and share ... [in a place where] we can say what we think, and explore those ideas' [staff]. Staff argued that because they were 'open to talk about religion [this] encourages students to think about what they believe themselves'.

I think I can express my [Hindu] faith because my friends are actually listening and find it interesting to find out about different cultures and the different festivals and things. (Student)

It's in the way that people look after each other and care for each other. It's in the way that this school has done things for its community and continues to do things, and the way that we support financially giving and just the moral encouragement, and just the decisions that we make – the way that we behave and the way we treat other people. (Student)

It is in these conversations about faith, in the classroom or outside, that students explored, questioned, challenged and reflected on the spiritual dimension to life. These conversations were made possible because of this sense of being a Christian community, a sense that 'runs through the veins of our school'. The relationships with people, students and staff within the school community enabled conversations about faith to 'just happen'. It is this sense of belonging to a community where talking about faith and belief could be the norm that enables young people to question, challenge, reflect and thus develop a greater understanding of faith matters and of their own spiritual identity.

The students in Bishop Justus emphasised the sense of a caring, friendly community:

82% – I want what is best for others

86% – My friends can rely on me

79% – I like to treat my friends

80% – I like the people I go to school with

Sustaining a sense of inclusive Christian community

> It is about listening, caring and collaborating; it is really nurture and it's that developing, growing, allowing people to flourish, that's good. It's a big thing . . . like that where it's actually lived. (Staff)

To return to a question posed earlier, how had a Church of England school established such a sense of community in a relatively short time frame? One of the main factors identified was a deliberate focus on the prioritising and making explicit of Christian values.

For example, hospitality was actively promoted, encouraged and supported within the professional community of the school. A sense of a welcoming inclusive community was strengthened by 'seemingly small things' such as encouraging all staff to come together once a week for tea and cakes at break. For staff to role-model the virtue of hospitality, inclusivity and nurture influences attitudes within the student community, but there is a deeper point to be made here – the school community is not simply the student cohort; all staff and students are part of one community, learning and spiritually developing together.

> So warm and welcoming, you know, one of the old phrases – open doors, warm fires – or something . . . it's that. (Staff)

To establish any sense of a cohesive community there needs to be 'ground rules for life' within the community. One of the essential elements of this is how the community deals with those who do not respect its rules and boundaries. For staff and students in Bishop Justus, it was clear that forgiveness was key to sustaining this inclusive community. The Christian concept of forgiveness is being highlighted in many English secondary schools now with the adoption of restorative approaches. A common misconception about this is that as a church school 'you'll talk a lot about forgiveness and people will get let off' (staff). In fact, it was 'tough love on occasions' (staff). (A more detailed consideration of restorative approaches is to be found in Chapter 10). A deliberate decision to make these and other Christian values explicit was taking place in the embedding of character education in all aspects of school life.

> That sense of community, [which] comes through in things like restorative justice . . . in the idea of forgiving and supporting. (Staff)

A sense of belonging to a Christian community

A Christian ethos cannot be imposed on a school, but is dependent on the contribution of all members of the school community. However, a sense of community can be nurtured, and a sense of the Christian nature of that community can be made explicit. Within this school several factors could be identified as sustaining a sense of belonging to a Christian community, including promoting values such as hospitality and forgiveness, emphasising an understanding of Christian community based on the principle of inclusivity, and prioritising and protecting time for daily morning worship.

Hospitality to strangers includes literal provision of food and lodging when needed, but it also goes well beyond that to a broader commitment to welcoming behaviour.[1]

This story of the Bishop Justus School has highlighted the impact that the careful design of collective worship has on the development of a strong sense of being an inclusive Christian school community. This chapter has shown how the careful design of collective worship embedded within a strong sense of Christian community itself contributes to strengthening a sense of community. It is, in fact, a virtuous spiral. The key question is, how is this embedded in a church school? Some of the levers put in place by Bishop Justus were a protecting of worship time; clear induction of staff into the purpose of morning worship; and review of the accessibility of worship resources and format.

sense of community

daily morning worship

stronger sense of community

Christians do not grow spiritually only by improving their understanding of Christian theology. They also grow by experiencing what it means to be part of a community that worships together, that practises forgiveness when someone is wronged. Such practices form the contours of a Christian community of faith, and by taking part in them Christians allow themselves to see and act in ways that resonate with Christian belief.[2]

A strong sense of belonging to a Christian school community influences spiritual development. The students described a school community where talking about faith was accepted practice and where believing in God was normal practice. It is a safe space to encounter, explore and reflect on religious experience. In Bishop Justus I had a glimpse into the experience of morning worship with a small group of students and saw how a sense of belonging may encourage spiritual development by creating a safe space where faith conversations happen and meaningful worship could occur. Major contributors to this were encouraging and making explicit Christian characteristics of community; promoting a clear understanding of Christian community as an inclusive 'togetherness'; and prioritising and protecting morning worship time.

```
┌─────────────────────────────────────────────────────┐
│ Chapter overview                                       │
│                                                        │
│   ●      Morning worship – making 'connections'        │
│                                                        │
│   ●      Faith conversations                           │
│                                                        │
│   ●      Sustaining a sense of inclusive Christian     │
│          community                                     │
│                                                        │
│   ●      A sense of belonging to a Christian community │
│                                                        │
└─────────────────────────────────────────────────────┘
```

Endnotes

1. Smith, David I. (2009), in *Learning from the Stranger, Christian Faith and Cultural Diversity*. Cambridge: Eerdmans.

2. What if Learning Programme: http://www.whatiflearning.co.uk/big-picture/background-research

5

Chaplaincy: sustaining spiritual development

Key ideas: chaplaincy; Christian service

Students in the Nottingham Emmanuel School said:

48%	God is very real to me
39%	I know that Jesus helps me
50%	I believe that God listens to prayers
37%	I am a spiritual person
45%	I am a religious person

NOTTINGHAM EMMANUEL SCHOOL (CHURCH OF ENGLAND)

Coeducational comprehensive school

11–18 years

c.850 students

Motto: Together to learn, to grow, to serve

> **The idea of faith journey is so interweaved with everything.** (Staff)

Spiritual development is like a journey; it is not a linear 'motorway', a moving from a to b. It is like a pilgrimage that twists and turns, and often involves a re-shaping, re-forming of the person undertaking the pilgrimage. The journey is an image that frames an understanding of spiritual development in the Nottingham Emmanuel School; it echoed throughout all my encounters with students, staff, parents and governors. Indeed, a question asked of all applying to work within this school community is: where are you on your journey of faith? Inseparable from the idea of life as a faith journey is the idea that life is about serving and helping others.

In the Nottingham Emmanuel School students and staff are actively involved in Christian service:

- It is not just being about raising money but being able to get your hands dirty and serving others. (Staff)

- Service is to do with being a rounded person, and from a Christian perspective that's what God intends for us to be and the school just helps by doing that. (Student)

- It's nice when you know you've helped somebody; it's a nice feeling knowing you've helped somebody on their journey with God. (Student chaplain)

- I do student chaplaincy only for one hour a week, because I've got so much to do, but it is the best hour of the week. (Staff chaplain)

Spiritual development for staff and students is about exploring and sharing your journey and leading others on their faith journey. This chapter explores two features in the Nottingham

Emmanuel School that contribute to this faith journey: the role of the chaplaincy as companions and guides on this journey and an understanding of a faith journey as being characterised by service to others.

An expectation of Christian service: 'Together to learn, to grow, to serve'

> The school logo is to learn, to grow, to serve. We do the logo. (Student)

Students in all the Ten Leading Schools were clear that spiritual development was not about what you believed, but about what you did; it is about serving others, and putting faith into action. The students in the Nottingham Emmanuel School drew my attention to their school motto, which is 'Together to learn, to grow, to serve'. They stress the importance of service to others as an example of the Christian values in school; this emphasis on service pervades school life. In the Nottingham Emmanuel School this Christian service is lived out in the school community, in serving the local community through helping with local projects, and in serving the global community, for example with links to Ghana and Sri Lanka.

This message of the importance of Christian service was echoed in collective worship and emphasised by all the year and house leaders (a house group includes students from all school years). For example, the year head began one Year 11 morning assembly with the Gospel story of Jesus washing the feet of the disciples. He went on to explain to the students the practical implications of the following week's Year 11 mock exams in school. He then linked the two by encouraging his students to recognise Jesus' act of service and suggesting that there was the opportunity for them 'in next few weeks to serve each other in time of exam stress'.

> When you look at it in the bigger picture [the motto] is what you need to do as a person and that helps you better yourself. You serve a lot of people, you get a reward from it and you're learning, you're growing, you're bettering yourself and you're bettering everyone else around you. (Student)

As in all the schools visited, the amount of time and effort devoted to charity fundraising is amazing; it is an accepted norm often not remarked upon by students or staff. The house system in the Nottingham Emmanuel School encourages students to be involved in acts of service and charity fundraising. These two aspects are kept separate so that the students understand the importance of 'serving others', of giving time and effort, not just money, to local charities or communities. This could be visiting old people, helping out in school as mentors, spending time at the food bank, or serving the school community as a student chaplain. Sixth-form students spoke of the many activities in which they were involved in terms of Christian service, such as acting as reading mentors for younger pupils; involvement and leading within local citizen groups; delivering acts of

> Obviously one of the Christian values is to give and help other people and I think that would be good to help the community even more. (Student)

> You feel part of something, you are always going to be needed – being here boosts your faith. Teachers are open with you; they share what they think. (Student)

worship and lessons in local primary schools; visiting the local hospice and delivering an afternoon of activities; learning sign language so they could serve other people; active involvement in Nottingham Citizens (a local social action group); and visiting a retirement home and putting on a talent show.

For these students, the expectation of serving others within the school, the local community and the wider community gave a sense of being needed by the school community and the local community. Many sixth-formers were expected to take a lead in these acts of service. For example, sixth-formers were leading a food bank project in a local primary school, arranging the logistics, communicating with the food banks, deciding how best they can support the food banks, and also leading in terms of encouraging the rest of their peers to be involved.

The students' responses in the survey reflected positive attitudes to Christian service:

73% – I like to spend time helping others

84% – My friends can rely on me

74% – I treat others the way I want to be treated

78% – I want what is best for others

The staff house leaders explained the rationale behind this emphasis on service. It was about encouraging students to understand that serving other people is more than giving financially. It is about 'giving up time or energy or prayer'. The house leaders spoke of it in terms of character education, of giving students the opportunity to develop the character trait of being 'servant-hearted'. If the students can really grasp that, they can begin to understand what it is to serve and to be selfless. The students reflected this back; some understood their role in school as to be one of service to others, so much so that when asked what they would change in school, one group of Year 9 students focused on how they as a school year should be more involved in helping the local community.

It is about emulating the life of Jesus and seeing that he came as a servant king, and therefore first to replicate that ourselves and to want to be servant-hearted ourselves. (Staff)

Staff and students pointed out that all students actively participated. Students enthusiastically volunteer to be involved in fundraising committees or social action teams, because 'they see it being modelled by their leaders and they understand the values' (house leader). The staff recognised that initially some students may be motivated by selfish reasons, such as something to put on a CV, or time out of school, but once they become involved their motivation generally changes.

Everyone is at a different point and spiritual development is like going on a bit further in that journey no matter where you're at. (Student)

Student chaplaincy team

In the Nottingham Emmanuel School the common language of the faith journey as a concept frames the staff and students' understanding and model of chaplaincy. This is a model of chaplaincy that sees chaplains as guides on that journey; the chaplains show the way, but also accompany people along the way, whichever way they are going. They do this by functioning as Christian role models, establishing deep relationships of mutual respect. Their visible presence in school and their focus on prayer, liturgy and service to others highlight these Christian practices in school.

> It's like you're on a journey and you have a map and the map is people . . . with you and so as you're going along your journey you're asking people for directions, what shall I do now?
> (Student)

> In Emmanuel chaplaincy is not a collar – [it] is really made up of all those different staff who in a bundle of different ways contribute towards the ethos and the life of the school and the enrichment life of the school.
> (Chaplain)

Chaplaincy within the Nottingham Emmanuel School resides not just in one person, but in a team of staff and students. The local vicar, who is a part-time member of this team, described it as chaplaincy with a 'fuzzy edge'. When he sought to describe the team to me, he spoke of a core of staff, including senior leaders. He then began to list the number of other staff who were involved in varying degrees, pointing out that many staff chose to work here to live out their Christian vocation. Recently, student chaplains had also become key members of this team.

The focus group interviews with students were often lively; students were keen to share their opinions and reflections on faith and religion. It was no different when I met with a large group of student chaplains from across the age range in the Nottingham Emmanuel School. They were eager to unpack the concept of student chaplaincy. They focused at first on what they were doing: producing, sharing and using a prayer book for Year 7 students and developing a resource for tutor worship. The tutor worship resource on the theme of Easter, on which they were working, was aimed at Year 7 and 8 tutor groups. The students explained that the aim was to teach about Easter in 'a fun, more interactive way' with games and prizes. They themselves had researched the story of Easter and considered a variety of online resources in preparation for developing their own material.

> We're working on a tutor programme for the Year 7s from the end of February half-term to Easter, about the Easter story and about how God saved us and things like that. (Student)

> There is a prayer book [in which] there's a section for family so there's a lonely prayer, there's a friendship prayer, loads of different prayers. And it fits perfectly in one of your inside [blazer] pockets. (Student)

The student chaplains gathered together weekly to 'talk about God' and 'to notice what God's done in our lives'. Their motivations for becoming a student chaplain were varied: for some it was a desire for knowledge and understanding, 'to know more about God, because I don't go to church every Sunday', to learn more about how 'God helps us'. For some who attended church it was a chance to learn about their faith in a 'fun way'. For others, it was seen as an opportunity 'to do something' about their faith: 'it's when you use your faith to help others'; 'it is about helping others on their faith journeys'.

> **It's a chance for us to gather together and talk about how we could bring God into the school more.** (Student)

> **[It is about] walking the journey with people but walking our own journey.** (Student)

A major focus of the staff chaplains' work in the Nottingham Emmanuel School was the lunchtime enrichment activities. Each year group approached this in a different way. For example, the focus in Year 7 was on games and films. In the older years more time would be spent in themed discussions. The Year 11s were currently working through a Church of England adult course book about being a pilgrim. It was a space and time for 'us to explore faith ultimately' (student). The older students were also encouraged to 'go out into the local community and do some service projects' (staff). The approach taken in all the year groups was to encourage students to think about how they put their beliefs into action.

Sustaining a chaplaincy team in school

Chaplaincy in schools takes many forms, even within the ten schools described in this book. Various models could be identified: chaplaincy as pastoral care, mentoring, as a form of youth ministry, as a liturgical role, as 'simply being', as a facilitator of Christian social action and charity work. In essence, school chaplaincy is not that different from other types of ministry in the Church: 'it is rooted in prayerfulness; it takes time and rests on the careful building of relationships; it enables the life of a community to be expressed and offered in worship; it is exemplary' (The Public Face of God, 2014).[1]

> **Chaplains are part of the essence of a church school, they embody and exemplify its ethos and they pray; they represent the place of God in the school and they represent the Church in the school and the school in the Church; finally they perform a role that is quite distinct from any others in the school.** (The Public Face of God, 2014)

School chaplaincy is such a vital ministry, yet it is often overlooked and hidden in school. The Bloxham research report on school chaplaincy[2] highlighted two really important findings: 'the potential impact of school chaplaincy on the lives of the young is considerable', and there is 'yet little clear, shared understanding of the nature of the role and accountability of school chaplains'.

The model of chaplaincy in the Nottingham Emmanuel School had been developed after much reflection and thought. A framework and various strategies were in place to ensure the large chaplaincy team worked together as effectively as possible.

Essential to functioning as a team was the weekly meeting involving all the key personnel. This enabled the team to be flexible and to adapt quickly to the daily needs of the school.

Another important element was framing the chaplaincy strategies and impact in the same format as the rest of the school policy documents. Reflecting on how the influence of chaplaincy could be measured, the chaplaincy team focused on 'narrative as a way of demonstrating impact'. The value of this approach was that the telling of the story of someone's faith journey in school influences all who listen and invites others to listen, and reflect; indeed, 'the telling of their story invites you to consider your own' (staff). Essential to effective chaplaincy in the Nottingham Emmanuel School was a continual virtuous spiral of reflection, trial, adaptation and more reflection.

> **Chaplains regardless of the model enter the marketplace and they hang around waiting to see where they're invited and then they work it out from there.** (Chaplain)

> **Just an hour a week at the start of the week with the key stakeholders means that we're on the same page when something comes up.** (Chaplain)

A theological interpreter

The model chosen by the Nottingham Emmanuel School is unusual; it offers up many more opportunities for chaplaincy work in school, but it also poses its own unique challenges. One of those challenges is the role of the ordained clergy in such a team; are they or should they be 'redundant'? Their role is obviously going to be different from that of being the sole chaplain within a school. Having chaplaincy run through all areas of school means that as a member of the clergy 'you perhaps contribute less to the pastoral side of chaplaincy' or to the preparation of worship resources. The challenge then is defining a distinctive role within the team. The chaplaincy team in Nottingham Emmanuel had reflected deeply on this issue and the local vicar, who was part of this chaplaincy team, had reframed his role as theological interpreter, with the purpose of developing the theological literacy of staff. This involved becoming more of a resource, with a greater focus on the 'nurture, encouragement of members of staff that are doing the hands-on delivery' (chaplain).

> **Midwife. Connecting. Interpreter. I was asked at some point to pick out three words that summed up how I saw my role. [It is] bringing to birth that which God is doing in any given place.** (Chaplain)

> **I find myself often in the place of being kind of the theological interpreter of what's going on and what we want to do and how that fits in with our understanding of who God is and what mission is about and what the kingdom of God is about.** (Chaplain)

The idea of the chaplain as a theological interpreter can perhaps best be understood by way of an example. In the Nottingham Emmanuel School, at the beginning of each staff in-service day there is a staff Eucharist. A recent in-service day had focused on the issue of raising the attainment of the poorest students, the 'pupil premium' students,[3] in educational terms 'narrowing the gap'[4] within school. In the Eucharist this was linked to the issue of justice in the kingdom of God; the prayers focused on the idea that 'narrowing the gap is about pursuing God's kingdom', that members of staff seeking to narrow the gap are 'unwittingly serving the purposes of God, or maybe even remarkably used by God for the purposes of his kingdom' (chaplain). This theme was echoed by the vice principal in the first presentation of the day, as he argued that the reason for focusing on narrowing the gap was because it was 'centred in the mission of a Church of England school'. This is a key example of the rooting of the educational in theology: the importance of an ongoing dialogue between education and theology and the value of space and time for that dialogue to take place.

> **I guess that's the prophetic thing of reshaping the thinking about the task of education.**
> (Chaplain)

> **What's going on in our church schools? Well, God is going on in our church schools; it's not a vacuum that we invite God into. God is already at work in our church schools so let's pay attention to what he's doing and unlock that.** (Chaplain)

The question raised with the establishment of a highly effective school chaplaincy team is whether the role of theological interpreter is an unnecessary luxury. The chaplain interpreted his role within the school not as bringing the message of the Church to school, or planning wonderful worship resources, but as recognising that God was already at work in this school, seeking out what people were doing in school and finding 'the incarnate God in the midst of it'.

Nottingham Emmanuel School is a school where chaplaincy is not hidden, and its influence on spiritual development within the school is considerable; the concept of chaplaincy is 'a golden thread that runs through everything; it is fully integrated' (chaplain). The opportunity to develop and sustain a large chaplaincy team within Nottingham Emmanuel arose through a coming together of many factors: people in key roles who wished to work collaboratively, and an established Christian ethos of service within the school. The latter facilitated the establishment of the staff and student chaplaincy team and influenced the chaplains' understanding of their role in school. The challenge of sustaining a large team of chaplains should not be underestimated. It is important to acknowledge that the structure of the chaplaincy ministry within Nottingham Emmanuel has not happened by chance, but has developed through careful thought by all involved.

Chapter overview

- An expectation of Christian service: 'Together to learn, to grow, to serve'

- Student chaplaincy team

- Sustaining a chaplaincy team in school

- A theological interpreter

Endnotes

1. Church of England Archbishops' Council Education Division (2014). The Public Face of God: Chaplaincy in Anglican Secondary Schools and Academies in England and Wales: https://www.churchofengland.org/media/2063650/nschaplaincyreport.pdf

2. The Bloxham Report (June 2011). Valuing the Unmeasurable . . . School Chaplaincy: what does research tell us? Project Papers 45: http://www.scala.uk.net/dyn/pages/research-project-report-for-2011-conference-2.pdf]

3. The pupil premium is additional funding for publicly funded schools in England to raise the attainment of disadvantaged pupils of all abilities and to close the gaps between them and their peers: https://www.gov.uk/guidance/pupil-premium-information-for-schools-and-alternative-provision-settings

4. Narrowing the gap – reducing within-school variation in pupil outcomes.

6

Encouraging inquiry

Key ideas: inquiry; form worship; religious education

Students in The Blue Coat School said:

42%   God is very real to me

44%   I know that Jesus helps me

47%   I believe that God listens to prayers

36%   I am a spiritual person

47%   I am a religious person

THE BLUE COAT SCHOOL, OLDHAM (CHURCH OF ENGLAND ACADEMY)

Coeducational comprehensive school

11–18 years

c.1,450 students

Mission statement: Faith, Vision, Nurture

> **The strapline is everything you can be and everything that you're meant to be.**
> (Staff)

As you walk up the drive to The Blue Coat School, Oldham the city of Manchester stretches out behind you, while in front of you stands an impressive nineteenth-century building, dating from the original school's inception in 1834. It is a school with a strong Christian ethos that permeates all aspects of school life – an intangible atmosphere that appears to the uninitiated to be transmitted in the air. Although students come to the school in Year 7 from a wide catchment area and many different primary schools, they express a strong sense of a school identity. In the spring of 2015, inspired by the hashtag #iambluecoat, form classes decorated a cardboard box with words and pictures describing the characteristics of The Blue Coat School student and 'what it means to be part of this school'. The boxes were subsequently assembled and displayed in the shape of a cross. The students' artwork identified the characteristics of The Blue Coat School student as being trustworthy, kind, open-minded, welcoming, loving, caring, well-mannered, resilient, friendly, having respect for others, aiming to achieve/support/practise/initiate change, willing to engage, questioning, and never giving up.

The Blue Coat School, Oldham is a school that combines a strong sense of identity with high academic expectations, where teaching and learning are valued and all activities are rooted in a Christian heritage. Within this context an emphasis on encouraging inquiry through Religious Studies lessons and collective worship is seen to make an important contribution to spiritual development.

Religious education, the Big Questions and the meaning of life

Where was God in the Holocaust?

A Year 9 Religious Studies (RS) class sits in silence as a sixth-form student recounts her recent visit to Auschwitz. As she draws her talk to a close, she is bombarded with questions not only about the philosophical and ethical issues, but also with questions about her feelings and her beliefs in the light of this experience. The students were being given the opportunity to explore in depth the question, where was God in the Holocaust? This provided a fascinating challenge for the Year 9 students and generated so many questions of their own. One student questioned whether the Holocaust was evidence that 'humanity had failed', another whether it could explain why people did not believe in God. Others grappled with questions arising from the argument of free will. They all were seeking answers, answers that would shape their own response to the question, where was God in the Holocaust?

For the students, RS was about being challenged by the Big Questions of life; it was a time for discussion, lively debates, an opportunity to express their opinion, but also a time to listen to the opinions of others. It was a time to be challenged and to challenge other people's views, and to try to understand 'why different people think different things'. One student explained that 'if someone didn't go to a church school they might just accept what their parents believe', but here in The Blue Coat School, they were challenged to form their own opinions.

> The Holocaust is the best topic that we've done because it is interesting ... it's relatable to today. (Student)

> Learning about [the Holocaust] can help us ... It helps you make up your mind if you do believe there's a God, and if you do then where is your religion, so you can make your own choice. (Student)

> Give [us] stuff to think about, give [us] scenarios or something that has happened and see how [we] feel about it. (Student)

> It helps you make up your mind if you do believe there's a God. [The teachers] give you ideas of what other religions are like and what they believe in, so you can make your own choice. (Student)

> I don't believe in God. In RS I'm learning about Hinduism and I can see sense in it. I think it's very strange how you're either one thing or another and you believe that your religion is right when there are many, many different religions. (Student)

RS is also about encounters with the other faiths and non-religious views present in the world today. The students reflected how RS influenced the way they formed their spiritual identity in relation to other religions and different ethical positions. The students were enthusiastic about this approach in RS. They held a flexible attitude to belief as they explored questions of identity and of belonging. They viewed RS as an opportunity to 'choose' or 'select' elements relevant for their lives. Discussions were seen to be 'open' with no right or wrong answers: RS made them think differently. Crucially, inbuilt into each RS lesson was a time to explore their own questions about matters of faith and to reflect on their response to these questions. These students revealed an understanding of religion that moved beyond the knowing of arguments for and against an issue, and key to this was the time to process how what they were learning about affected their personal beliefs and practices.

The approach identified by the students had been intentionally built into the RS syllabus. It was an approach that had been recognised with the award of the Gold standard RE quality mark.[1] Key elements were challenging and encouraging the students to question; modelling a range of responses; and time for reflection.

The programme of study focused on religious, philosophical and ethical questions, challenged students to think about specific questions, to consider different examples from different faiths, and required them to respond with their own questions. This method required students to develop a questioning approach; for example, often in lessons all students had to identify the questions the topic had raised for them.

[Students do not] have to have a faith to develop spiritually; they can still think about big questions and consider the meaning of life. (Staff)

The value of modelling a range of different responses was important. Effective RS enables students to understand that there is little if any agreement about the right or wrong answers. All staff in school were open to talk about their faith and their opinions, and this diversity of opinions was drawn upon in RS lessons. It was about modelling a way of thinking and encouraging students to reach a conclusion about God and spirituality.

I'll often say this is what so-and-so said, or I tell them stories of people that I know… They are having it modelled to them, [shown] that a range of responses is ok. [It encourages] them to think, I can say what I think because of this. They'll often stay behind after the lesson to tell me how they feel about it. (RS staff)

If you let people think about it in their own way, then they'll make their own decision and they won't be influenced by anyone else. (Student)

The other key element to this approach was deliberately making space for 'thinking time' in all lessons, even into the examination classes at Key Stage 4. This provided students with the time and space to think about 'their spirituality, whether they had a faith, and the impact that this has on their life' (staff). It provided the necessary time for students to process and think through issues, questions and challenges to their beliefs, and a time to be open to new ideas and concepts.

If you don't give people time to process it then you're just wiring their brain up, aren't you, and they just close down because it's all a bit too much. [They need] a bit of quiet time during the day. (Staff)

One consequence of this is the developing of skills of inquiry, enabling students to engage with, question and be challenged by religious concepts and the spiritual dimension of life. It is developing skills so that students can interrogate and interpret religious phenomena and evaluate their relevance for their own spiritual identity.

Religious education and spiritual development

A focus on inquiry in RS makes a positive contribution to spiritual development. It enables students to reach informed conclusions about their opinions and beliefs and to be able to question and engage in dialogue with others. If the Religious Studies syllabus is construed to provide a safe space to encounter, explore and reflect on religious experience, it is a space where skills of inquiry can develop, where debates can ensue, and a quiet time for reflection can take place.

> **Religious education contributes dynamically to children and young people's education in schools by provoking challenging questions about meaning and purpose in life, beliefs about God, ultimate reality, issues of right and wrong and what it means to be human.[2]**

Within The Blue Coat School RS is considered an effective contributor to spiritual development. In all ten schools, students emphasised the contribution that RS (or RE) made to their spiritual development. However, some RS teachers view RS as an academic subject, and religion, ethics and philosophical issues were studied as such; for others, RS as a subject is distinctive and is a major contributor to students' spiritual development within schools with a Christian foundation. The experience of RS within The Blue Coat School demonstrates that the conflict between RS as an academic subject and RS as a major influence on students' spiritual development is a false dichotomy. RS can be a subject with strong academic rigour while also one that makes a contribution to students' spiritual development by challenging their beliefs, encouraging them to question and giving them time to reflect, to shape their spiritual identity.

It is not only in RS that there was space and time to discuss religious issues. Students 'did religious stuff' in many other subjects. For example, In RS and Art students worked on 'religious art', producing paintings of the stations of the cross and an Easter-themed display. Students and staff in The Blue Coat School pointed out that throughout the school faith was talked about, and you could talk to anyone, 'not just a select few'. As the head teacher explained, there was 'no embarrassment when we talk about God' or faith or the Christian concepts of love and redemption.

> **The atmosphere in this school means that you start to get a lot more involved in questioning what your beliefs actually are.**
> (Student)

Form group worship

What I like about worship at Blue Coat is that they manage to break it down so it's easier to take in and people can understand it easily. (Student)

A time each day when this 'faith talk' was prioritised was in collective worship. Collective worship within The Blue Coat School is active: it is throwing a globe around in assembly, playing noughts and crosses on stage, eating a mini chocolate egg and saying prayers as it melts in your mouth, discussing big issues such as guilt and death, and standing up to defend your opinion. It is a whole-school service in the local parish church with the school's award-winning brass band performing. It is also a time for discussion and reflection with the form class: a style of worship appreciated by students across the ten schools.

A good thing about form time is that each form takes its own approach; it means everybody has their own twist on it. (Student)

You don't have to see things to see it's beautiful. (Student)

We are all beautiful, made in God's image. Allah doesn't judge you on your outward appearance but on your hearts and deeds. [I learnt that] in RS from the Qur'an. (Student)

We were asked some questions like what type of thing we felt was beautiful. (Student)

One week in March 2015 form worship focused on the question, what is beauty? The resources, prepared by the school chaplain and shared with all staff, included questions about the nature of beauty, a reference to Genesis 1.27 – the idea that all are made in the image of God – and two video clips: one with blind people talking about what they find beautiful and the other about a door labelled 'for beautiful people'. Each form approached this in different ways. Some worships were student-led, but all involved intense discussions on the nature of beauty. Two teacher-led worships took two different approaches. In one the lively discussion was stimulated by the question of whether, if all are made in God's image, he sees everyone and everything as beautiful. In the other the debate focused on how the media portrayed people and the impact this had on their self-esteem. A Year 8 form produced reflections on the many different forms beauty can take. In Year 7 enthusiastic students led their peers in interactive games and then reflected on how hearing what blind people thought of as beauty had changed their own ideas about what was beautiful.

The students' responses to this worship were interesting. In the previous weeks, the themes had been about death and guilt, topics they had also found challenging. For the students, worship provided not only some thought-provoking moral challenges; it was also a source of ethical guidance, guidance that was relevant to real life, about how to 'live your life, to be a good citizen, relate to different people'.

It provided an opportunity to encounter Christianity in a way that was accessible to all. As students pointed out, collective worship always contained 'some link to God and/or Jesus'. It also provided them with space to question and challenge beliefs and practices.

It is about teaching us the right from the wrong and how we can get over that if we have done something wrong, how we can overcome that and make things straight. (Student)

For example, [one was] about what love is, with quite a few biblical teachings. Sometimes there's a video done, usually by Christians. [The teacher] will talk about God and how it's related to them, then they will ask about our opinions. (Student)

Having the same form for four years you get to know the people in the form. The stories you may contribute to the [worship] is not something you should be embarrassed by. I think the more you know people, the better form worship can be, because then you can talk about things that you've done or experienced and you can work from that. (Student)

It's community as well. You're in a safe environment and people around you are helpful and you know they're going to guide you in the right direction in the future. (Student)

Form time could be such a space because of the relationships developed within each form between teacher and students and between students – the sense of community. Several staff likened this to a sense of being a family. Worship time was a demonstration of that family coming together, of 'that very strong sense of family, so whatever background the young person comes from they know that they're part of that'. For the students, form worship was valued and appreciated because it was worship with a group of people known to them, where they could raise difficult questions, share personal experiences, listen to others, and participate fully in discussions.

Form worship is a coming together in a small group. It is accessible; it is interactive; it is a thought-provoking question or statement; it is a lively discussion, where others' opinions are questioned and treated with respect; it is a closing moment of reflection.

Offering positive experiences of collective worship

I'd call myself a Christian but I'd also say I was atheist at the same time. (Student)

The Blue Coat School chaplain had identified several distinct groups of students within the school, such as:

- Students from a non-religious background or other faith traditions.

- Overtly Christian students, keen to be involved in worship in school.

- Students with an active faith, a good support network from their churches and youth groups, but who were reluctant to be involved in worship in school – 'they come to school to learn and they want to keep [faith] separate'.

- A sizeable group of students who were nominally Christian but saw worship as a 'negative thing'.

The students held a variety of understandings of what it meant to be Christian in a church school, but they appreciated the openness of worship. One student who identified himself as a Christian atheist explained that he didn't feel pressure to believe in God – in fact, being part of this school meant that 'you're allowed to be your own person'.

An aim in developing and preparing collective worship in school is to engage all students, but a challenge is how to engage students with negative attitudes to worship. From the chaplain's perspective, it required a constant attempt 'to break down some of the barriers that they've got towards church'.

I think that God has never really done anything for myself, because I just don't follow the religious practices that are Christian like praying and stuff like that. (Student)

I don't know, but I think God's real but I think there's more to just God, there's more outside of death and stuff. (Student)

[Worship is] different, more of a happier like interactive feeling, rather than if you go to church [where] it's a bit like solemn really. (Student)

In The Blue Coat School one way of addressing the needs of this group was through developing worship material that was engaging, encouraged interaction, and challenged students to deepen their knowledge and understanding of a spiritual dimension to life. One way that proved fruitful with this group of students was to present them with different and positive views of Christianity, demonstrating that, as a faith, it was more than their previous experiences of church and liturgy. For example, worship time offered the opportunity to encounter a variety of styles of worship, some with formal liturgy, others much freer.

Providing a diversity of approaches allows students to learn about the different liturgical styles, and also enables students to encounter a style that engages them, depending on their experience or preferences. Students appreciated the variety of styles, some preferring more upbeat songs to hymns, others the formal liturgy in the parish church setting.

The service in the school hall on Friday for the younger years will be quite informal. There will be games in it, the songs will be fairly up to date, with the guitars and the drums playing the music. The service will be in the church for the seniors and the music department lead the music, so it's much more formal. The band will be playing. And that's a real contrast between the two styles.
(Chaplain)

It's communication, it's reiteration, it's modelling. You've got to have good people doing worship.
(Head teacher)

Key to the success of such an approach is ensuring that all people delivering worship have a positive attitude to its importance and value, and that it is overseen by someone who is 'imaginative and creative', who understands the students' needs and can develop engaging worship throughout the year.

The approach of The Blue Coat School, Oldham to collective worship recognises the need for a safe space to worship, a sense of belonging to a community; a space in which worship can be thought-provoking, will challenge students with complex and controversial moral issues, and will enable encounters with a diversity of Christian practices and beliefs and liturgies.

Chapter overview

- Religious education, the Big Questions and the meaning of life

- Religious education and spiritual development

- Form group worship

- Offering positive experiences of collective worship

Endnotes

1. For further information on the RE quality mark (REQM) see website: http://www.reqm.org/

2. The Religious Education Council of England and Wales (2013), A Curriculum Framework for Religious Education in England (p.11):
   http://resubjectreview.recouncil.org.uk/media/file/RE_Review_Summary.pdf

7

Enhancing theological literacy

Key ideas: theological literacy; Christian scriptures

Students in Tenison's said:

76% God is very real to me

78% I know that Jesus helps me

74% I believe that God listens to prayers

64% I am a spiritual person

75% I am a religious person

ARCHBISHOP TENISON'S CE HIGH SCHOOL, CROYDON

Coeducational comprehensive school

11–18 years

c.800 students

Motto: Academic excellence in a Christian community

At the end of a busy morning, in the middle of Archbishop Tenison's CE High School hall, students hurry to lunch or extra-curricular activities and a few staff and students gather for a short service of midday prayers. As the noise subsides and everyone reaches their destination, we listen to the biblical story of Daniel's struggles in the lions' den (Book of Daniel, chapter 6). Every day as the bell tolls for lunch, this time of quiet reflection takes place. This practice of midday prayer began in the midst of Tenison's 300th anniversary celebrations, a time of jubilee. In the Bible a jubilee year is a time of doing less, when small but significant things become important. Small but significant is key; what people here often mention as important are small gestures such as saying hello in the corridor, the smile when you are having a bad day, or making the time for prayer.

We've gone back to the roots. Maybe that's the image, from the Old Testament where they are told to re-dig the wells where things had gone dry (Genesis 26.18). Under the head's leadership we've re-dug those wells to select the fresh water back in again. (Staff)

Developing a Christian education relevant for the twenty-first century presents a challenge and even more so an opportunity for this school with a rich 300 Christian heritage. This chapter focuses on how scriptural and theological literacy contributes to students' spiritual development in this school.

Theological literacy of Christian students

Tenison's was unique in the group of Ten Leading Schools in that the majority of students could draw on a rich experience of an active Christian faith in their home and church; indeed, the Christian faith played an important in their life.

All students and staff emphasised the strength of the sense of a community of Christians in school. The students perceived the staff as Christian role models. One student explained how he was supported by having teachers who were Christian, as that encouraged him 'to say yes, it's possible I can live a good lifestyle, I can live a Christian lifestyle'. Another highlighted the 'sense of whole community spirit' which developed from being a Christian school, and 'helped to keep my faith going'.

> I reckon myself as a Christian... because I've experienced God in my life.
> (Student)

> There's a prayer group which meets in the hall at the start of lunch every day for five minutes. I feel that's the influence; it's not in your face but it's definitely just there pushing you along. (Student)

> I pray not because I have to but because I want to.
> (Student)

The students openly discussed the experience of God in their lives, and their involvement in church activities. They spoke about a faith passed on in the family, and the value of prayer in everyday life. Several students mentioned morning and evening prayers, grace before meals, and family prayer time. One student explained that, in fact, prayer just occurred 'when I feel like I want to communicate with God – I will just do that at any time really'.

> Their weekends are dominated by church; the students spend Friday night in a church youth club, most of Sunday and then part of some Saturdays [in church activities]. (Staff)

All students and staff emphasised the strength of the sense of a Christian community in school. Many also pointed to the challenge that this posed, highlighting the diversity of expressions of Christianity within school. In 2015, 42% of students coming into Tenison's came from an Anglican church background, 10% were community places, and the other 48% were drawn from a wide variety of churches: Catholic, Baptist, Pentecostal and others such as the Redeemed Christian Church of God, Jubilee Church, Christians in Action, and Restoration World Revival. Discussing church attendance with a group of Year 9 students revealed the complexity and the variety of their family backgrounds. Many 'belonged to' at least two different denominations, occasionally three. Several students referred to themselves as Pentecostal and Anglican, identifying elements they liked in Pentecostal worship, like 'the vibrancy', and in the

Anglican, which 'in a way takes it a bit more seriously; [it is] more spiritual'. The different church congregations that the students belonged to were not necessarily in the same town; some explained that they and/or their families kept changing churches to find one with which they 'were comfortable'.

Theological literacy and an educated faith

However, the complex religiosity of this student community provides many opportunities and gives rise to different challenges for a church school. This diversity sometimes posed a challenge in terms of collective worship, as both staff and students recognised that there was 'a slight disconnect' between the students' experience of worship in a more evangelical church and the school Anglican tradition.

The head teacher identified that a clear challenge for a church school is to establish the role of the school in the spiritual development of students who 'already know they have a relationship with God'. He argued that the church school should be encouraging these young Christians to form questions such as:

- What did they want to do with their lives?

- How did their faith connect to the real world?

He interpreted this depth of religiosity in the students as a challenge and an opportunity for Tenison's to develop in these young Christians an 'educated faith', not uninformed, or unwise or naive about the world.

Just as cathedrals are built to enable people to encounter God, theological literacy enables pupils to encounter the fundamental concepts upon which religions are based; it debates them and considers how they relate to each other.[1]

For the head of Religious Studies (RS), this complex religiosity opened up opportunities in the classroom. Such a diversity of expressions of Christianity provided a richness of theological ideas. For example, in one classroom the majority of students could proclaim themselves Christian but have very different views on different issues. In the Key Stage 3 curriculum, in addition to Religious Studies focusing upon study of Christianity and other major religions, the Year 8 and 9 students studied a lesson of theology once a week.

Invited in to observe a theology lesson, I was totally surprised by the lively enthusiasm with which the Year 8 students debated the Arian controversy. The students did not approach this as some dry theological argument, but as a real question to be solved. Was Jesus eternal, or was he 'just' a good man?

The head of Religious Studies (RS) had deliberately built into the theology syllabus interactivity and drama, and students actively engaged with this approach. In the interviews the students shared their enthusiasm for theology, speaking over each other as they described what they did in theology lessons.

Arian controversy: this was a big question for the church because if Jesus was not eternal then he was not fully divine. If Jesus was not divine the church would have to stop worshipping someone who was not God. (Teacher's notes)

In theology we're learning soteriology. It is all about salvation.
(Student)

The Year 8s start with looking at what God is like. It is understanding theology through story, so we also look at the nature of the Holy Spirit and we look at the life of St Paul. The students themselves asked us to do some eschatology. (Staff)

In computer science, we have the chance to rewrite the curriculum. I've deliberately embedded at each stage so many links with creation, because the creation of a game is really creation of, like, a universe. So really getting them to think about the big questions. So we ask questions like, is knowledge innate? Is there a designer? We look at computer scientists like Charles Babbage, who was one of the inventors of computers, and he was a committed Christian. (Staff)

The students enjoyed the study of theology; eschatology and the Book of Revelation were particularly popular with some of the students interviewed.

Theological literacy is not confined to the RS department. For example, several students drew my attention to recent assemblies when a teacher from each department had come and spoken about why their subject is important and how it relates to Christianity. The head of geography had spoken about the creation and stewardship of the world. Theological literacy is embedded throughout the school curriculum. Tenison's is a school with high expectations of academic success, and seeks to ensure that this academic excellence is situated within the Christian ethos.

Developing theological literacy within a church school is important for students who come from a Christian background. Many students in Tenison's pointed out that school was often the only place where they had the opportunity to develop a questioning, intelligent, wise faith. In their places of worship, they were either 'side-lined' into children or youth groups where questions of faith were 'dumbed down' or sat in the mainstream liturgies without the opportunity to ask questions. This was highlighted in responses of a group of sixth-form students:

- Before I came to Tenison's it was just, oh Jesus came, he died on the cross. But when I came here it was emphasised why it happened and why it's important, so it gives a greater understanding.

- I think I'm a Christian now, with a lot of questions. I do believe in God and I believe in Jesus and all of that, but I do have a lot of questions about where we came from. I focus in life on helping people and trying to be a better person, and I don't know, just fulfil the roles of a Christian.

- It helps me to stick to my faith, I don't just get misled. Because I learn things at church on a Sunday, but if that's backed up by everything I learn at school as well I stay on the right path, if that makes sense.

A member of staff reflected that the school was developing young people, young Christians, with a deeper understanding of their faith, who appreciated that they had a role to play in society, that life was about what you can contribute in terms of service. His views were echoed by many sixth-form students, who detailed the many charity activities the school and they were involved in. As one student pointed out, 'it's just heavily emphasised that there's more than just us – there's so many other people that you can help'.

> **Helping others gets very emphasised. I like doing things like helping with charities and helping others has definitely helped to keep faith strong.** (Student)

Enhancing scriptural literacy

Once a week senior leadership team meetings start with a reading from the Bible. Teachers from other schools listen in astonishment when Tenison's staff explain that they spend perhaps a quarter of an hour of their weekly meeting reading a passage from the Bible. At the time of the research the senior lead team were working their way through the Acts of the Apostles – not as a Bible study class, or devotionally, but looking to what it said to them as leaders in a church school.

> **We reflect on [the Bible passage] and relate it to what's happening in our school at the moment and the challenges we face ... I am a cultural Christian, I'm not a practising Christian, but [reading the Bible] in school every week. It is a time of learning and developing.** (Staff)

This Bible reading at senior leadership meetings was mentioned by all staff as evidence of the Christian ethos of the school; it also signposted an emphasis on developing scriptural literacy that pervaded the school curriculum and collective worship.

The use of the Bible in collective worship is common in many schools, with the choosing of verses or stories to highlight a particular issue or theme. In Tenison's the approach taken to the Christian scriptures is different. It is an holistic view of the Bible, not just a selecting of particular stories or verses. A member of staff described it as a thoughtful approach, 'grounded in a real world application of Christian faith'.

Each assembly moved beyond a basic knowledge and sought to deepen students' understanding of the Bible and of biblical characters. Staff and students emphasised that the assemblies were 'quite deep' and definitely not simple messages like 'we all need to be nice to each other'. One student described assemblies as 'a time of learning, because most of us don't really read the Bible as much as we should'.

Ruth, I liked the Ruth one; it just showed that women can be independent and make their own choices and she just, even though she was married to someone powerful, she showed that she had the power to make her own choice. (Student)

One assembly gave a three-dimensional understanding of a character like Peter. It went into depth about human failing, temptation, decision-making and needing to stand strong, and when you've messed up getting up again.
(Staff)

**Honestly, when I heard [the story of Job] before it was a summary about how someone had so much and it got taken away but he was still loyal, but hearing it in further detail [today] was really good.
I think to me the deepest point was where his friends were encouraging him and yet discouraging him.** (Student)

I listened to an assembly on the biblical story of Job, which looked at the depths of Job's suffering, considered the meaning of true friendship and reflected on the relevance of the inclusion of the Elihu speeches in the Book of Job. I was interested in the students' response to this analysis of Job. The students already 'knew' the story of Job. One student linked it back to a discussion she had had in her RS lesson, when she had considered whether Job would have felt any different if Satan had not applied any one of those tests of Job's faith in God. Many students reflected how hearing the story again in assembly had 'deepened' their knowledge.

> **When I developed the scheme of work I thought this could be quite dry, but then I thought no. The Bible isn't dry, the Bible is quite exciting and actually it's because of the narrative and the story within the Bible that really brings across the theological message of what God is like.** (Head of RS)

> **A more positive attitude towards the Bible is associated with a greater level of biblical literacy. RE is crucial here, because more pupils cited RE as a source of biblical knowledge than any other source and it is the only situation in which every child in the UK is inducted into 'theological' discourse about biblical narratives.**[2]

A comprehensive focus on the Christian scriptures in school was a deliberate decision of school leadership. The aim was for students to encounter the scriptures in a holistic manner and to develop skills of interpretation and engagement with the Christian scriptures.

In Tenison's the Religious Studies curriculum has been so structured that at Key Stage 3, in addition to Religious Studies, students study biblical studies in Year 7. It is in biblical studies that the students explore the scriptural text in depth, not only hearing the stories but interrogating the biblical text.

Students also encountered the Christian scriptures in other areas of school life. Tenison's run yearly retreat afternoons for young people to develop 'ownership' of their faith; or, as the chaplain explained, to be taken out of 'their bubble' and think about faith for themselves. The retreats were based on the Bible verse for that particular year. The verse for Year 9 was 'ask and it will be given to you' (Matthew 7.7). Each retreat had a similar format: a walk to the local church, eating of lunch together, a short worship followed by a carousel of team-building activities, prayer station, a guided meditation and a discussion on their Bible verse.

Tenison's students were confident in interpreting the text and expressing their opinions about scripture. They had an in-depth knowledge drawn not only from school but also from reading the Bible at home. Several had their favourite books of the Bible.

> **The retreats were a good way of getting people to think about how the Bible is relevant to their stage of life but also to think about what it means and where they can take it.** (Chaplain)

> **I really pick [the Bible] up to read Psalms because I think a lot of Psalms are helpful in life as well.** (Student)

Tenison's approach to enhancing scriptural literacy emphasised the idea of development, of 'stretch' in spiritual development. Students were encouraged to delve deeply into the meaning of scripture. It is an approach that moves beyond an understanding of scripture as needing to be 'dumbed down' for young people; it moves beyond listening to a Bible story to find the moral, and beyond the view of Bible verses as mantras for moral guidance. It views the Bible as a text written over 2,000 years ago, which requires an understanding of context, but which needs to be read in its fullness, interpreted and reinterpreted for each generation. The holistic approach taken by Tenison's offers many opportunities for students to encounter scripture and to engage, interrogate, interpret and question the texts.

'Do you understand what you are reading?' Philip asked. 'How can I'?' he said, 'unless someone explains it to me?' [Acts 8.30–31]

The Bible doesn't stop the minute they put a full stop in, because there is this gap, the gap we're filling at the moment, so actually our story becomes important when we place ourselves within that grand narrative that's there. (Head teacher)

You can't get to the end of a day here where you haven't been pulled into prayer, reflection, reading of a biblical passage. (Staff)

To encourage a mature understanding of the Christian scriptures and concepts and to prioritise enhancing scriptural and theological literacy does make a contribution to students' attitudes to the Bible and to their understanding of Christianity. Religious Studies is a key area where this can happen but, as the story of Tenison's demonstrates, this should not be the only area in a church school where it can happen.

A key factor highlighted by the story of Tenison's is the importance of educators being aware of the students' faith journey and recognising that, as in all areas, the role of the Christian educator is to challenge and stretch students so they do fulfil their God-given potential. If students come into school with an active Christian faith a church school has a role to ensure that they develop an 'educated faith'. An 'educated faith' cannot develop in a vacuum; it should of necessity take into account 'the real world' – and students at Tenison's were keen to stress that they were not living in a bubble. Spiritual development for these students was taking place in a world in which they had many personal, academic and global concerns. It was a world understood from within the framework of the Christian faith, but a faith that was questioning, wise and intelligent.

Chapter overview

- Theological literacy of Christian students
- Theological literacy and an educated faith
- Enhancing scriptural literacy

Endnotes

1. Chipperton, J., Georgiou, G., Seymour, O., and Wright, K. (2016), Rethinking RE: Religious literacy, theological literacy and theological enquiry: http://reonlineorg.wpengine.com/wp-content/uploads/2016/02/REThinking-RE-REOnline.pdf

2. Copley, C., Copley, T., Freathy, R., Lane, S., and Walshe, K. (2004), On the Side of the Angels: The third report of the Biblos project. Exeter: University of Exeter Press.

8

Encouraging Gospel values

Key ideas: Gospel values; prayer; chapel

Students in St Joseph's said:

54% God is very real to me

58% I know that Jesus helps me

61% I believe that God listens to prayers

42% I am a spiritual person

49% I am a religious person

ST JOSEPH'S CATHOLIC AND ANGLICAN HIGH SCHOOL, WREXHAM

Coeducational comprehensive school

11–16 years

c.750 students

Mission: St Joseph's is a shared faith school which strives to guide the whole school community to achieve their full potential, grow in their journey with God, and live a Christian life, which we will do in Christ's love, by the example of St Joseph, the Worker.

Often when visiting a school for the first time, it is common practice to be given a tour of the premises by students. St Joseph's Catholic and Anglican High School, Wrexham was no different. The tour this time was undertaken by an enthusiastic Year 8 student. James* was a confident young man who had 'done' many school tours, and was determined to show me the whole school. As interesting as the tour of the buildings was, it was James's commentary that gave an insight into life at St Joseph's. As we went in and out of lessons James was welcomed by name by all staff as he explained the importance of each subject. When we wandered into the empty chapel, he drew my attention to the beautiful artwork on the walls, produced by students and the chaplains. He shared how he had come to the chapel on the anniversary of his 'Nan's death' and had written a prayer for the prayer board. He pointed out the anti-bullying box where you could slip a note in, and Year 11 students will follow up any issues.

We seemed to come to the end of the tour of all the buildings, but James decided there was one last place we needed to go – that is, the school playing fields. While we walked I questioned why we needed to see this, suspecting this may be a tactic to delay a return to lessons. James was adamant that it was essential because I had been asking about Gospel values. He wanted to show me how they permeated all aspects of school, including PE, where 'we are taught to play with compassion for our opponents, we care if someone falls over on the opposite side'. On our walk back across the field, I asked which of all the Gospel values was the most important for him. He answered quickly and simply, 'Faith, because without faith there is nothing.'

This glimpse of the school highlights the themes that weave through this institution and this chapter: Gospel values and the inseparable, interwoven strands of chapel and prayer.

'Gospel values are built into us'

One Wednesday in spring 2015, I was invited into a selection of lessons in St Joseph's. That it was a Wednesday was of interest, because Wednesday was 'Welsh Wednesday' when every lesson included words of Welsh woven into the lesson and spoken by teacher and students. However, of more interest to me was that also woven into each observed lesson were Gospel values.

A selection of examples from observed lessons:

History (Year 8): Identify the Gospel values shown by the Cavaliers and Roundheads, noting similarities and differences.	A heated debate ensued as to whether both sides could show **faithfulness** to God's will.
Art (Year 9): Identify integrity and gentleness in today's lesson.	**Gentleness** in the way we treat each other, for example when James showed me how to draw hands. **Integrity** in the honesty in which we approached our drawings.
English (Year 10): Read a short critique on the death of Curley's wife in *Of Mice and Men*; identify the Gospel values the writer has shown.	Students highlighted the attention drawn to the **compassion** shown towards his wife, the **forgiveness** shown for the cruel things she had done and **humility** in the understanding of why she did them.

The Gospel values were very visible in St Joseph's, displayed on classroom walls and in planners. The values were also heard in the language used by staff and students and modelled in encounters in the classroom, in worship time and in the corridors. Students had clear opinions on which value was must important for themselves:

- **Justice** – it says a lot about the school because everyone gets on and it considers the world as well.

- **Kindness** – no school is going to work properly unless everybody is kind and tolerant of each other, and cooperating.

- **Tolerance** – it is needed in lessons when people don't pick things up as fast as other people.

- **Compassion** – we all have to respect each other and love each other and be kind.

- **Forgiveness** – if something happens in school and it upsets you we can all forgive.

- **Gratitude** – just because: it is being thankful for each other, being thankful about the school and our families.

Each new generation of students was introduced to the Gospel values in RE lessons, assemblies and in form time. For example, each form has a patron. There are five in total: Maximillian Kolbe, Oscar Romero, Sheila Cassidy, Sean Devereaux and Martin Luther King – twentieth-century Christians chosen by a previous generation of students as Christian role models. The example of these patrons is used to show the students people who were motivated by and lived out the Gospel values.

> **With the form patrons you get really inspired.** (Student)

Students were quite adept at identifying the values in each lesson and aware that the values were so embedded in the life of the school that teachers did not need to 'point them out'.

> **The Gospel values show us how we perceive people who may be less fortunate or are different; they help us respect them.** (Student)

The students in St Joseph's are eager to share their understanding of what the Gospel values are and how they could apply them to a variety of subject areas and situations, in their life inside and outside school, now and in the future. The Gospel values became part of them, gave them confidence to 'be themselves' and gave them the confidence 'to know what's right and wrong, to stand up for others'. One student argued that Gospel values should be taught to everyone, 'not just for people with faith but for people who are atheists as well or agnostics or whatever, I think it's important for anybody'.

> **The Gospel values have created the people that we are. The Gospel values that we have help us respect ourselves and make us think before we do things that could either hurt us or somebody else.** (Student)

The influence of Gospel values such as integrity is apparent in the students' responses from the whole-school survey in 2016:

86% – Others can trust me to be fair

80% – I am honest with others

85% – I can be trusted to keep my promises

96% – I try to treat people fairly

Modelling Gospel values

A key question is, how have Gospel values become so deep-rooted in the daily life of St Joseph's and accepted by staff and students as the norm? One factor that could be identified was staff awareness and ownership of Gospel values.

> **Most [teachers] have their Gospel values displayed. We selected a number of Gospel values, we have them on cards with a definition or explanation of what they mean. We try and incorporate one or more of the Gospel values in as many lessons as we can.** (Staff)

> **I'm a maths teacher and I'm often referring to my Gospel values wall when they're doing things like group work. We relate that to tolerance and respectfulness. We relate it to parts of the lesson, whether that's the design of the lesson or whether that's the topic of the lesson.** (Staff)

The staff explained that the aim in each lesson was to encourage and model Gospel values, to display Gospel values somewhere in the classroom and make explicit the incorporation of one or two Gospel values in as many lessons as possible.

Each teacher had their own method of incorporating the Gospel values into their subject and into the lesson. The embedding of Gospel values in teaching and learning is carefully monitored and supported. For example, it could be a focus for lesson observations; or a professional development target could be to incorporate Gospel values more fully into one's teaching practice. Senior leadership encouraged the teachers to try to make visible all the values, not just 'the easy ones'. However, incorporating Gospel values into all lessons explicitly was not always easy. The lesson structure might not lend itself, or the values might become implicit in the lesson plan rather than explicit. However, staff were keen to emphasise how modelling Gospel values throughout the whole curriculum was important and that this was a clear expression of the Christian ethos of the school.

An interesting aspect raised by several staff was the influence modelling Gospel values in their daily life in school had on their own life and values outside of school. For some staff, embedding these values in their professional life resonated with their personal values; for others it was a challenge; and for some, working with Gospel values daily had influenced the development of their own values and faith.

> **The Gospel values play a massive part in my life. But it wouldn't have done so had I not come here.** (Staff)

Prayer

Prayer is an active and powerful part of the life of the school. (Head teacher)

Gospel values permeated daily life in St Joseph's because it was a school with an emphasis on faith, on prayer, 'with Christ at the centre' (head teacher). At the heart of St Joseph's, both physically and metaphorically, is the school chapel – a space for prayer, for quiet and for reflection. In Christian-ethos schools with a chapel or chaplaincy space this is often a key area that sets the tone for the nature of spiritual development within a school. A brief glimpse of activities in the chapel gives an insight into the prayer life of this school.

In St Joseph's the chapel is an L-shaped room with posters on the wall with biblical quotes and beautiful calligraphy completed by students, and the altar sits in the centre. On the wall near the door is the prayer board. Across from this is a space for students to leave their shoes as they enter this space. Early one morning the chapel provided a quiet space for Anna*, upset over the illness of her mother. At morning break someone may come in to write a prayer and post it on the prayer board, or just to sit quietly.

> **When I came in Year 7 I didn't really believe. I now pray every night. I come into the chapel and ask the chaplain to say a prayer for me, because I don't know what to say. I get so much support I never don't want to come to school.** (Student)

Once a week at lunchtime the chapel becomes a place of worship for a form class Eucharist (Anglican or Catholic), where the students do all the readings and prayers. As the Mass ends the students leave all their readings and prayers in front of the altar, where a pattern of coloured ribbons and branches are arranged. Another day that same week the chapel is the venue for lunchtime prayers; in front of the altar lies a wheel made with ribbons, all colours of the rainbow. The chaplain shares modern-day images of the Stations of the Cross and encourages the young people to write/draw their own prayer. As they write, the young people discuss needs for prayer in the world and in their lives. During the day the chapel may be the venue for an RE class – for example, a Year 9 class came in to reflect on those in prison over the coming holiday. They filed quietly into the chapel as music played in the background and sat on the floor cushions. The chaplain lit a candle and all made the sign of the cross and said the prayer in Welsh. The students reflected on the meaning of some artwork produced by those in prison, then the short 'service' finished with a prayer and the class returned to the RE classroom.

Once a term, at the end of the day, a group of staff meet for prayer in this space. Recently, St Joseph's has begun the practice of staff prayer every Friday morning at 8.40. 'It is absolutely beautiful and really well supported; nearly all staff attend weekly' (staff).

> **The thing I really liked and was impressed by was staff prayer. Last time I was feeling a bit stressed by everything, but it was so lovely sitting in the chapel before Lent. It was just a bit of time ...** (Staff)

For the students in St Joseph's the chapel was inextricably associated with prayer. Prayer takes many forms: formal prayer, both teacher-led and student-led in collective worship, and the Eucharist; informal prayer in worship and on the prayer board: verbal or non-verbal, written or drawn. It was a rich pattern of prayer and attitudes to prayer that was found in St Joseph's.

> It's harder to think where prayer isn't in it! It's in the air we breathe really, isn't it?
> (Staff)

> Prayer permeates everything that we do. The children see participation in the religious life at school as something that they're proud to take part in.
> (Staff)

> In my form class they'll just pray from whatever words come into their heads. Some will have it pre-prepared. Quite often the children will bring in a newspaper article that's moved them in some way and they will want to reflect on that. (Staff)

However, encounters with prayer were not confined to the chapel; they also occurred in collective worship at the beginning of the day and at the end of the day. Listening to students and staff discuss the role and importance of prayer in school provides an interesting glimpse of the nature of the Christian ethos of this school.

Morning form worship is a time of reflection and prayer. Every classroom has a prayer focus board, a bank of resources and a candle used for form worship. The students make the sign of the cross and say the prayer in English and Welsh at the beginning and end of worship, candles are lit as part of a stilling/centring exercise, and students write or research their own prayers relevant to the theme of the week. They are encouraged to participate actively and take responsibility; 'it's not something they sit in silence and is done to them'. For instance, there is a prayer rota for morning prayers – the students will lead two or three minutes of morning prayer and take responsibility as worship leaders. At the end of the day there is a specially written prayer and in some departments there are prayer ambassadors in each class who take over the last five minutes at the end of the day.

Developing a prayerful culture

> [Prayer is] more a numinous thing; it's not really to do it for regulations or to look any good, it's really to build the individual's being and connection with God. (Student)

The emphasis in St Joseph's was not just on acceptance and encouragement of prayer, but also on developing the prayer life of students and staff. Key to this development is the work of the chaplains. They are role models for prayer in school and focus much of their efforts on empowering students and staff to develop their own prayer life.

Prayer was approached through art and through stilling exercises with pebbles, bulbs and paper boats. The chaplains highlighted the influence of training students in stillness techniques, giving the students space and opportunity to 'open up' to prayer. In reconciliation services students are encouraged to explore non-verbal ways of praying, for example 'picking up stones, or washing stones clean'. Simple acts like removing shoes before entering the chapel instil a sense that this is 'holy ground', a sacred space, and encourages 'the respecting of the sacred in one another makes the whole action, everything physically they do, part of the prayer, not just the words or anything written down' (chaplain). Students are encouraged to create their own personal prayers, or prayers to share with their peers.

An effect of this is the thought-provoking prayers that students share in their worship time and the acceptance of prayer as part of daily life.

> **We made a little boat and then we wrote on it. It went into the water and then the water rubbed the pen away from it. So it's a way of saying that bad things go away.** (Student)

> **It puts your life into perspective just to pray because although you're not getting an answer it gives you the feeling that someone is there and actually listening to you. And I feel like it's a personal thing and it's just between yourself and God so I just find that it helps you spiritually.**
> (Student)

Different, but together witnessing our faith

An awareness of the Christian faith underpinning the school is enhanced rather than diminished by the joint Anglican and Catholic nature of the school. From induction in Year 7, students are required to reflect on their faith position in relation to their denominational status, but also to their relationship with the Christian faith. A joint school is involved in continual reflection and negotiation with regard to governance and faith practices in school. The St Joseph's chaplaincy had an added dimension, with three chaplains contributing to the chaplaincy team – an Anglican vicar, a Catholic sister and a Catholic priest. In working together each brought their own gifts and talents and established a well-respected chaplaincy in school. For the students, the emphasis was on a shared common Christian faith, with an awareness of different interpretations; 'the only thing that separates us, it's just who drinks the wine and that is literally it' (Student).

> I'm an agnostic, I'm on the fence, I wouldn't say I'm particularly a Christian. It's just the experience, being able to refocus, and the people I've met have shaped who I am and it's an experience. I'd never forget this school. (Student)

> I think we've got something beautiful here, you can't really express and explain. Because obviously we're all different denominations but we get on so well and I think it does inspire pupils by seeing us and witnessing to our faith, that has a profound effect on them.
> (Staff)

> [Spiritual development is] about encounter. It's making sure that children encounter Christ in people. It's a very transient population so you are constantly renewing, recreating what it means to be a community. You're constantly revising that engagement and ensuring those encounters happen, those Emmaus moments. (Staff)

The chaplains argued that the joint nature of the school made them all more aware of the authentic nature of faith. It demonstrated how real faith was for them and for the staff. For example, in the eucharistic celebrations (alternately Anglican or Catholic), when the students saw that some received the bread and others didn't, it showed the reality of faith in daily life – not perfect, but real and meaningful. It was also important that the chaplains and staff were not 'apologetic' but clear about what they believed and where they stood. The common consensus was that the visible presence of the two denominations within St Joseph's was a positive element, not confusing for students but rather emphasising the importance of faith, beliefs and practices.

St Joseph's is a school with the focus on explicit Christian values (Gospel values), Christian places (the chapel), practices (prayer) and people (chaplains). There is an awareness that each of these could be seen through a secular lens, the values being good values for any human being, prayer being a useful stilling or calming exercise in a busy school, and the role of chaplains as pastoral counsellors. However, in this joint Anglican–Catholic school each of these aspects is viewed through the lens of the Christian faith, not only by school leadership and governance but also by staff and students. The students appreciated this Christian focus and many argued that their faith developed within the ethos of this school. This explicit Christian lens is a key to a positive contribution to spiritual development.

An explicit Christian ethos does not just happen by chance. One important element of the St Joseph's story is that the explicit Christian lens, the encounters with Christ in people, cannot be taken for granted. The population of any school changes quite dramatically each academic year. New students and new staff need to form a new community, to reinterpret Gospel values, and to experience and encounter sacred space and practices of prayer. The deliberate decisions and intentions of leadership, staff and chaplains with St Joseph's are crucial – for example, the prioritising of Gospel values, and the monitoring and support offered to all staff. Role modelling and offering and developing a variety of approaches to prayer means Gospel values remain at the forefront of school life for each new generation of students and teachers. For some it will reinforce values and practices from outside school; for others it will be a novelty and a challenge. For all it should be an opportunity to form and shape their own spiritual development.

Chapter overview

- 'Gospel values are built into us'
- Modelling Gospel values
- Prayer
- Developing a prayerful culture
- Different, but together witnessing faith

Endnote

* pseudonym

9

Modelling Christian inclusivity

Key ideas: family; Christian role models; inclusive community

Students in the Oasis Academy said:

31%	God is very real to me
28%	I know that Jesus helps me
31%	I believe that God listens to prayers
31%	I am a spiritual person
31%	I am a religious person

OASIS ACADEMY, COULSDON

Coeducational comprehensive school

11–16 years

c.930 students

Outstanding – Everyone Every Time

The Oasis Academy, Coulsdon is a learning community formed on the concept of a family: a family that works together and has the highest expectations of all its members. It is an academy that is characterised by inclusivity and the celebration of individual differences.

> **We are family. We have family leaders, family groups. Most people have form groups, but for us it is the word family.**
> (Student)

It is essential to understand how important a sense of 'family' is within the Oasis Academy, Coulsdon. On my first day in the academy, Jack* was eager to explain to me what was so special about his school. He believed it was because it was like a family, where everyone could rely on each other. Indeed, he suggested most students chose this school because they liked 'the sense of a community and a family'. His friends agreed with Jack, pointing out the close relationship they had with their 'family' leader, and members of their 'family group' in school.

The focus in this chapter is on the ways in which this sense of family is interpreted in the Oasis Academy, Coulsdon and the contribution it makes to the spiritual development of all students.

The Oasis family

The Oasis Learning Trust, of which the Oasis Academy, Coulsdon is a part, has a clear vision of how the Christian ethos expresses itself in its school. The Trust has a Christian foundation 'motivated and inspired by the life, message and example of Christ'. The Oasis Learning Trust academies are not faith schools and have totally open admissions criteria. The Oasis Academy, shares the Oasis Community's vision for education as it is expressed in five statements:

- A passion to include everyone.

- A sense of perseverance to keep going for the long haul.

- A commitment to healthy and open relationships.

- A deep sense of purpose that things can change and be transformed.

- A desire to treat everyone equally, respecting differences.

These five statements shape the Christian ethos of the Oasis Academy, Coulsdon, and exploring each of these within this chapter highlights the key features that contribute to spiritual development in this academy.

A passion to include everyone was expressed in the strong sense of belonging, the prioritising of the value of community, and in the language used in this school. The sense of perseverance resonates through the embedding of character traits in the Oasis Academy, Coulsdon. A commitment to healthy and open relationships and the deep sense of purpose that things can be changed is found within the role modelling of values within the school community. A desire to treat everyone equally, respecting differences, is demonstrated by the example of the academy's O-Zone unit for students with autistic spectrum disorders.

An inclusive family: a desire to treat everyone equally, respecting differences

An example that reflects the strength of the concept of family, the inclusiveness in this school, and the influence of developing character traits on students' attitudes and behaviour is the O-Zone unit. This is an integrated unit in the Oasis Academy, Coulsdon for students with autistic spectrum disorders. It is a separate space within the academy, to which only students who are part of the O-Zone have access. It is used for small classes and individual support for students. It is a safe space to which these students have access at any time of the day.

The other students interviewed were proud of this aspect of their school. They shared their understanding of autistic spectrum disorders, the challenges these pupils faced and the ways in which they were accepted within the mainstream school.

The staff within school had made a deliberate decision to inform all students about the nature of autism and the challenges these

Oasis is not trying to pretend it's something it's not, it's saying this is what we are and this is what we believe in and if you want to come on this journey with us, come in. (Principal)

I just think it's so powerful for the other students to be aware of difference and disability and tolerance and patience. It sounds a bit corny that you're going to educate the next generation but it really is. (Staff)

I have a girl in my year, she likes to come into some of our classes but if she feels that in lesson maybe she needs a little bit more help then she will go to the O-Zone. (Student)

students face. Resources are sent to all tutor groups; the occasional assembly will focus on autism and all students at some stage attend a workshop in the O-Zone on autistic spectrum disorders.

The staff in the O-Zone highlighted how the mainstream students were very accepting of and patient with their students, perhaps instinctively, but also because they now had themselves a greater understanding of autism. A member of staff working in the creative arts had noticed how integrated the students with autistic spectrum disorders had become within that class, partly because the other students readily helped them. When she had thanked one girl the previous week for the extra help she had given, the girl had responded with just, 'Well, why wouldn't I?'

Another student had pointed out that when a supply teacher had told a student off for doodling in class, the rest of the class had risen to his defence and explained why he needed to doodle. Often the students were the best advocates for the autistic students. The students identified the O-Zone students as individuals with individual differences and needs. The students reflected an acceptance of diversity and a valuing of being an inclusive family community.

The sense of all belonging to one family where individual differences are recognised, supported and celebrated has a positive benefit for the O-Zone students themselves, who often arrive in school with low self-esteem and an acute awareness of their difference.

A positive acceptance of difference presents a very powerful message to students who often have not had previous positive experiences of school. The notion of family, which pervades the whole of the Oasis ethos, is brought into play here. In the O-Zone the day begins and finishes with all the students together listening and sharing their experiences of the day. For the staff this is important as it 'grounds and centres' the students; it develops a sense of being part of the O-Zone family. However, students also experience a sense of belonging to a wider family group, in that they will be involved in the family (house group) assemblies and activities. The O-Zone staff

> **It takes a while for the tolerance, especially because some of the behaviour of our students is quite subtle and their disability might be quite hidden; they might not look like they've got a disability. So again we're very open about who we are and what autism is.** (Staff)

> **They teach us; the way [autistic pupils] perceive the environment is different from how we would perceive the environment and they get upset by things that we wouldn't necessarily get upset over. That's why a lot of people struggle to understand autistic people. It has helped me have a lot more understanding and respect in that sense because if you don't understand you're very naive and you just make judgements upon it but because I understand it more I guess I am more tolerant.** (Student)

> **We have here pastoral care for the individual child – it is perseverance and inclusion that really happens here.** (Staff)

highlighted how these students felt accepted and welcomed into a school family that is so inclusive and nurturing.

A passion to include everyone

The idea of viewing the school community as a family had been a deliberate decision in the early days of establishing the Oasis Academy, Coulsdon. Traditionally the school, like many others, had had year leaders. When senior leadership and staff reviewed this structure, they decided to change and chose to implement a framework that would enable the students 'to feel more part of a family within the school and the community as well'.

The principal stressed the importance of this sense of being an Oasis family, within the academy and in the international context of Oasis. The concept of the family was chosen to 'help students adjust when they come in Year 7'. In practice, in the Oasis Academy, Coulsdon there are several levels of this school family, the smallest being the mentor group, which is year-based and consists of groups of about 18 students. Each mentor group then forms part of a 'family group' made up of mentor year groups from across the key stage. The next level up is the whole school Oasis Academy, and ultimately it includes the whole of the Oasis family across the world.

This sense of family was very important to all the students interviewed. It generated a strong sense of belonging and a sense of togetherness. Many students said that the family structure made them 'feel comfortable' and welcomed, with a sense that you could 'rely on each other'. This sense of being a family carries with it certain beliefs and values and character traits. The principal explained that he shares with the students that as a family together, 'we'll need to be resilient, and we'll need to be loving towards one another'. One student drew a connection between being a family and Christian values, as being a family in school was about 'people working together', and not being selfish.

Integral to the principal's understanding of his role was the concept of family. The school community was like a family that shares and models the same values, rooted in the Christian faith – a 'family' where

We're a real community in the O-Zone and we support each other. There is that sense that they're very much part of the O-Zone and that we're a family within ourselves but we're also very much part of the DaVinci family as well and part of the Oasis family. (Staff)

I'd say the spiritual side is more of bringing in the family sense. The whole ethos includes the love, care and family. (Family leader)

I think the families are really important, the fact that we talk about family a lot and we talk about this Oasis family. (Principal)

I think Oasis is the whole community, the whole we're-together thing, like you're not alone. You can talk to people. I just think it's the whole sense of a family really. (Student)

everyone looks out for each other, and where every child has 'an advocate' – someone to speak up for them. The principal drew attention to the wider reach of this understanding of family: the Oasis Academy, Coulsdon is part of a much larger Oasis family, and students were very proud of this connection to a much larger international Oasis 'family'.

Character traits: a sense of perseverance

Within this framework of belonging to a family, the Oasis Academy, Coulsdon promoted the values necessary for young people to flourish individually in a family community together and in the wider world. In the spring term of 2015, the students drew my attention to the Oasis values. The school had identified character traits that would help the students to succeed academically and become 'outstanding, socially conscious and responsible citizens'. The character traits then were aspiration, grit, self-control, love and zest. They were everywhere throughout the academy: on posters on the walls, in the language used in the classrooms, in collective worship and in pastoral care. The students all claimed that they not only knew the values but applied them in school and in their life outside of school.

Examples of the character traits could be found embedded in teaching and learning. In a post-mock exam biology class, Year 11 students were reviewing their papers and highlighting the trait that they would require to improve the result they had just achieved.

In a GCSE English class students were analysing which of the character traits were visible in the passage in *Of Mice and Men* by John Steinbeck they were currently studying.

Students themselves drew attention to PE and creative arts subjects as places where they most often saw the character traits expressed by staff and other students. In school, developing these character traits was seen as aiding students' learning and their behaviour.

> **Grit** is knowing that you want to stop, but knowing you should keep going and sticking at something even though it might be hard or you find it difficult or boring or you really don't want to do it but knowing it will help you and making sure you keep going with it. (Student)

> The teachers really push for you to have these character traits and to use them in your day-to-day life. If you're messing around, literally all that they have to say is **self-control** and you just know what it means. (Student)

> I think like zest in the cooking sense … **zest** is just having that extra something at the end little bit, just that extra little push. I think a lot of teachers talk about zest for learning because if you want to learn you're obviously going to do better. (Student)

> I think **love**, I mean tough love because love comes in all types of situations. Like for example, if you're doing a fitness test in PE and you're really doing bad, then the teacher will [say] you're better than that. That's tough love because they believe in you. (Student)

Indeed, several of the older students pointed out how much better behaved their year group was than the Year 7 students who had not yet learnt the character traits.

> **Students' responses to questions about the value of aspiration:**
>
> 93% – I have high hopes for my future
>
> 92% – I want to be successful in life
>
> 89% – I want to do my very best in school
>
> 88% – I want to make the most of my life

For the students, these character traits were also relevant outside school for their everyday life and their future. They stressed how developing and building up these traits would prepare them for the future and help them face unknown situations in the outside world.

The character traits were under regular review by the school leadership team. In 2015/16 it was decided that character traits that had been very relevant for the academy when it opened had now become so accepted by students that some new traits were needed to further challenge these students. The leadership team reviewed the possibilities and came up with a list of around ten. These were then shared and discussed with students and staff in assemblies and meetings until a consensus narrowed them down to five.

The five new character traits were: belief, love, creativity, integrity and perseverance. The leadership emphasised that students are introduced to these new character qualities through teaching and learning, collective worship, and consistent role modelling. One member of staff spoke of how the character traits 'rubbed off' onto the students, and in her Year 11 class she could see how the ethos has been embedded in the students' attitudes to each other, in work and in helping others.

They talk to us all the time about how we should aspire to be the best we could be. I know there are quite a few people from my primary school who didn't really have any goals, but having the aspiration trait made them think, I need to come up with my own ideas and my own pathway to where I want to get to. So I think it made us all think about what we want to do, how we want to get there a lot more. (Student)

We've always taken the opportunity to celebrate them when you see them but also pulling them up where you don't see it and actually trying to educate the student and staff member in that. We can be very explicit in unpicking that here and we talk a lot about holistic education. (Principal)

We retained love – because what would we be saying if we took that away? The head emphasised that all are known and loved; sometimes, though, it is tough love. (Staff)

Role modelling: a deep sense of purpose that things can change

A key feature of the Oasis Academy, Coulsdon was the role modelling by all staff of these character traits. A member of staff, when explaining the importance of the concept of family in the school, stressed that for students who maybe lack positive role models in their family at home it becomes important to have people around who will model positive choices. In character education one of the key features that contributes to the spiritual development of students is the role modelling of character values.

All staff aimed to express these traits in their relationships with the students and to be role models who consistently offer clear rewards and clear consequences and set clear boundaries. The staff also stressed that it was important to 'celebrate' and compliment the students when they saw they expressed the character traits.

Within the Oasis Academy, Coulsdon students and staff highlighted the principal as a key role model. Staff emphasised that the decisions he made were made with integrity and in line with the character traits of the school and that he provided 'proper spiritual guidance'. Staff and students spoke of the 'meaningful' way that he prayed for and with them.

The principal himself was well aware of his place as a role model, as a spiritual leader for the school community. He framed his understanding of this role within a Christian context; for him, being a prayerful presence in the community was important. He often used the phrase, 'your life will often be the only Bible people read', so it is crucial that it is the 'right kind of book they are reading'.

> **Example is a good thing really; if you've got the example from the head downwards, they are thinking along those lines.** (Governor)

> **As the principal I'm very much the one that sets the weather, sets the tone, and obviously in that role I'm leading, so I'm leading by example, and really setting the direction of the vision, the way the vision's going.** (Principal)

> **My mentees notice that [the principal] prays differently. It is seen as real and from the heart – he never reads a prayer; he is seen as authentic. Prayer is very inclusive – he pitches that prayer to be inclusive – at the right level.** (Staff)

The ability to live out one's faith in work was a concept that many teachers in Christian-ethos schools share, and for the principal it was important that there was no dissonance between his life as a Christian and what he said and did in school.

Staff commitment to the Oasis ethos often meant going beyond the everyday, developing meaningful relationships with students and sharing a sense of 'bespoke' care for the individual. Many expressed a deep sense of purpose that things can be changed; many held a view of the transformative power of an education based on a Christian foundation.

The sense of family and the promotion of the character traits create an inclusive environment in Oasis Academy, Coulsdon, in which students' spiritual development can flourish. Spiritual development is expressed in the five statements underpinning the ethos of the academy: a passion to include everyone; a sense of perseverance to keep going for the long haul; a commitment to healthy and open relationships; a deep sense of purpose that things can change and be transformed; and a desire to treat everyone equally, respecting differences.

But for me the authenticity of my faith and what I'm saying need to go together. I need to be true to what I believe and it happens that as a believer that's what I need to express. (Principal)

I feel that the importance of the Christian ethos runs through Oasis Academy, Coulsdon. (Principal)

Chapter overview

- The Oasis family

- An inclusive family: a desire to treat everyone equally, respecting differences

- A passion to include everyone

- Character traits: a sense of perseverance

- Role modelling: a deep sense of purpose that things can change

---

Endnote

* pseudonym

10

Prioritising reflection

Key ideas: reflection; restorative approaches; sacred space

Students in Bishop Luffa said:

36% God is very real to me

39% I know that Jesus helps me

41% I believe that God listens to prayers

39% I am a spiritual person

41% I am a religious person

BISHOP LUFFA SCHOOL, (CHURCH OF ENGLAND TEACHING SCHOOL), CHICHESTER

Coeducational comprehensive school

11–18 years

c.1,400 students

Mission statement: Always our best because everyone matters

Many view spiritual development as being characterised by grand emotions of awe and wonder. However, a theme running through this book has been that often the features that influence spiritual development in Christian-ethos schools are the little things, the hidden things. In Bishop Luffa School it was the moments of silence that hinted at a key feature that contributes to spiritual development in this school:

It is about creating opportunities to touch that spiritual bit of young people, to touch that bit, the cornerstone of their faith, to actually experience, tie in with all of that stuff, experience of God, knowing who they are. (Staff)

- The long silence in an interview, as students search for words to describe their visit to Tanzania, a 'life-changing' experience that is beyond words.

- The quiet moment when a teacher and student sit together and reflect on restoring justice in a certain situation.

- Students seeking quiet contemplation in the 'Quiet Place', a garden built in memory of students who had died.

Creating a school environment in which spiritual development of all students may flourish is a challenge for any school. Bishop Luffa School is a place where time and space for quiet reflection have been created in imaginative ways, and where reflective practice flourishes in a climate of compassion and openness to diversity. This chapter explores the times and spaces created for quiet reflection and considers how the school environment shaped by the school mission statement – 'Always our best because everyone matters' – contributes to spiritual development.

Providing space for reflection

In all schools, space is at a premium. Even finding a free quiet space to conduct interviews is a challenge. Having a space in school that is dedicated for quiet reflection, an area of sacred space within school, is often an impossibility. Bishop Luffa addressed this challenge in a most imaginative way by creating an outdoor sacred space within the school grounds. The 'Quiet Place' is a piece of land that runs along the school boundary; it is now a space used for reflection by individuals or classes. It is an imaginatively designed garden, originally created after the death of two students.

It was designed by a sculptor in residence working with the students to create a space for private, personal or class meditation time and it is designed in such a way so that a whole class can sit around a central cross. The design was inspired by the idea of a journey, the twists and turns becoming a metaphor for a spiritual journey. To ensure that the meaning of the Quiet Place is not lost with each new generation, the Religious Education department have included visits to the Quiet Place within the syllabus. At times of crisis or tragedy students find their way to this place for quiet moments of reflection.

The space for reflection can also be found outside the school boundary. In all ten schools staff and students spoke of the powerful effect of taking students away from school for retreats or reflection time. In Bishop Luffa the history teacher drew my attention to this effect within history trips. He regularly took students to visit the World War One battlefields and the World War Two Wannsee Conference centre. In the quiet time of reflection in front of the graves, or in the room where the Final Solution was decided on, the students would 'respectfully stop and think', and then reflect deeply on the implications of what they were seeing, and begin to understand and grasp the enormity of the experience. Each year the students held a short religious ceremony in the cemetery at Tyne Cot, Belgium, laying a wreath, saying a prayer, taking a moment of collective reflection. For the staff this was part of acknowledging 'we are a church school'.

> The Quiet Place became its working title and it stuck. When we were getting close to opening the Quiet Place every child in the school was invited to write a message on the back of a pebble, a prayer or reflection. (Staff)

> If you walk over there you'll see for yourself, it's a very special place. It's a real asset to the school. It's quite exceptional, very special. If you were to walk around there you would see what I mean. (Parent)

> The German cemetery, Langemark – in many ways that's even more powerful than Tyne Cot. The pupils there are even more affected because there's mass graves there and it's much more defeatist, it's much grimmer. It makes lads who can sometimes swagger and have bravado actually just stop and think. (Staff)

> You could just send them in to [Wannsee] and they just disappear and get totally absorbed and you can see their moral outrage, their moral shock. (Staff)

In the sixth form there's spiritual spaces. The library gives a little pack, once a week. In the corner it has like a spiritual theme. This week it's about the child throwing the starfishes back into the water. (Student)

There was one with a display of flowers where they had mirrors shining off so you could see it from different perspectives. When you actually put it into more of an interesting or different perspective, it becomes easier for young people to develop spiritually than to be sat in church. (Student)

It does help to build bridges ... I think the very fact that we're a church school and it's about justice and moving on. Sometimes it is just that things have broken down and it's in everybody's long - term interests to rebuild those bridges. (Staff)

There's a lot of things which sometimes you don't always feel are tangible; the way in which we're using restorative approaches with young people, a sense in which you're trying to be inclusive and recognise that we're not perfect and that we're trying to grow together. (Staff)

The space and time for reflection can also be created within a classroom, at a particular time and place. A challenge for many Christian-ethos schools is how to contribute to the spiritual development of students in the sixth form. Often the sixth form will bring in students from other schools, who may not have experienced a Christian-ethos school previously. There is a different mix of students and a different response is required. In Bishop Luffa, they have made a decision to allocate a time once a week, in tutor time, which they have called 'Spiritual Spaces'.[1] This is a time when students can think, reflect, discuss, talk, share, be creative and be silent, go deeper into matters of faith and raise questions. The programme has been devised with set resources prepared by a small team, including representatives from the sixth form. The aim is to find ways in which the sixth form can continue to access the spirituality of quiet time.

The majority of students and staff interviewed emphasised the value of this space and time for reflection in school: the value of having a space where they may 'digest', process and reflect on the impact on their own faith, beliefs and values.

Time for reflection and reconciliation

An issue faced by all schools is how to support students when 'things' are not going well, when they are challenged by or are challenging the rules of the community. In Bishop Luffa they have focused on the benefit of time for reflection and reconciliation and have developed a process with inbuilt time for reflection.

Restorative approaches, sometimes called restorative justice or restorative practices, are a method that is increasingly employed in many schools. Restorative approaches encourage all involved to reflect on their behaviour, take responsibility for their own actions, and work for reconciliation.

In Bishop Luffa the restorative approach is framed within the concepts of truth and reconciliation. It allows students a chance to tell the truth, to understand how their actions have affected other people, to know that things can be forgiven, and to appreciate forgiveness. The process is straightforward and follows set pathways. Both parties respond to the five questions:

1. What has happened?

2. What were you thinking about at the time?

3. How were you feeling at the time, and what are your thoughts about this?

4. Who has been affected by this?

5. What needs to happen to make things right?

Restorative approaches are employed in situations of conflict between students, between students and staff, and between staff. Often the impact from taking a restorative approach is greater than the usual forms of punishment such as detention; although staff point out that at times it has not been easy to convince some students and parents that it is not a soft option.

Bishop Luffa School identified the clear benefits it brought to many aspects of life in a church school. Several staff thought that restorative approaches were a good illustration of the Christian ethos of the school. Restorative approaches, with the inbuilt Christian concepts of reflection, forgiveness and reconciliation, is now the norm within pastoral care and behaviour management in school.

One member of staff reflected on how it may influence the development of young people's conscience, this sense of reflection on what has gone wrong, seeking forgiveness and reconciliation. This helped a growth in their understanding of who they were, what their values were, and how they integrate that into their understanding of self and in their interactions with others in the community.

You hear them say 'I'm sorry – this is what really happened' when we have restorative meetings. (Staff)

I don't think [the ethos] is just about morals in a secular way. I do think it's about all of these issues of forgiveness and justice and equality and things that are fundamental tenets of Christianity. (Staff)

It's really important as a teacher myself to model being a Christian person, [in] many ways, like restorative approaches. I pray with children on occasion; the power of that is phenomenal. (Staff)

Restorative approaches seem to work very well and I think that it affects their spiritual being and helps them to grow and react and respond and respect one another. (Staff)

> It gives them a chance to tell the truth and understand that things can be forgiven and appreciate forgiveness. It's hard to forgive somebody unless you've really thought about how it's affected them. (Staff)

> Reflection happens in lessons. We work very closely with children about how they learn, what's your best style of learning ... and that comes out of reflection about how best you learn. (Head teacher)

The fact that this process was so established was due to it being prioritised by senior leadership. They ensured that all staff had undergone training in this process so that they are all confident in holding 'restorative conferences'. This in turn meant that all staff are modelling in school 'how we deal with conflict, how we deal with hurt and wrongdoing' (staff). This role modelling influences how children themselves approach issues of conflict. It also provides a 'shared language and an agreed practice' for resolving any conflict in school.

Students did not use the exact term 'restorative approaches' but rather spoke of the concepts of reflection and forgiveness in school. For example, at one student council meeting, the students were reviewing the wording of the school's drugs policy, and the issues they raised with regard to the punishments detailed focused on their concern as to whether there were sufficient opportunities for forgiveness and reconciliation or rehabilitation of the offending student. The example of restorative approaches in school is evidence of how this culture of quiet reflection is embedded in Bishop Luffa School.

Other areas where this practice of reflection was found and encouraged was in collective worship time and in teaching and learning. In the latter, all staff were encouraged to be reflective practitioners, and students were encouraged to reflect on the ways in which they learn to identify their own particular learning style. In collective worship, time was being built in for contemplation or quiet prayer or meditation. The student worship representatives and staff were supported in developing this by the worship coordinator. Making space for times for quiet reflection can be daunting in a classroom situation, and often it needs to be modelled by the staff or students leading worship for it to develop successfully.

> **Student responses to statements about forgiveness:**
>
> 73% – I readily accept an apology
>
> 80% – I allow others to make a fresh start
>
> 70% – I own up to my mistakes
>
> 85% – Others can trust me to be fair

'Time for inquiry; a time to push the boundaries' (Head teacher)

Establishing a school environment where the practice of reflection is encouraged in all areas of school life behaviour, actions and beliefs is made possible because of the school culture that emanates from the school motto, 'Always our best because everyone matters'. In Bishop Luffa, this school culture is characterised by an openness to an expression of a diversity of beliefs and practices.

For many students the climate they identified as necessary for spiritual development was one of openness. It was the creation of a space where you were 'free to challenge', to question your own and others' faith, a space where there was 'open discussion' that leads everyone to a clearer understanding of their own development.

For many students this space and time was found within their RE lessons. It provides a space and time when students could 'learn to articulate' what they believed in, 'without offending others' (student). The students were very clear that spiritual development was not about what 'people believe'. Indeed, they often explained that it was a good sign that they or their classmates had come to the conclusion that they were agnostic or atheists; it showed that religion was not forced on you in this school and was evidence that students had developed their own views: 'people had made a decision for themselves' (student).

Many of the students and staff interpreted the contribution of the Bishop Luffa School to spiritual development as providing these opportunities to encounter the spiritual dimension of life.

The school was able to provide time not found elsewhere in their lives for students to 'talk about faith, belief and things like that', developing a particular 'thought process' that encourages students to think differently, to think more deeply about the spiritual dimension of life.

> The school isn't a monolithic culture; it allows room for all people to grow as individuals and all of their views, even if they're a bit teenage reactionary! But they're encouraged to discuss things and figure out their own way through. (Parent)

> [In RE you] can look at an issue and say, how does my faith apply to this? How does it fit into the world? Across the school generally, but especially in RE, you really have the opportunity to talk openly about an issue. (Student)

> It's that whole idea that people are happy to ask questions of themselves and what they believe in and what matters to them beyond transient things. It's the idea the students understand that there's more than just what they see in front of them, that there's more to life, that there's a greater power at work than just themselves. (Staff)

Time to care 'because everyone matters'

The other aspect of this school culture that staff and students identified as contributing to their spiritual development was the Christian concept of compassion. Care for each other and efforts put into charity work were features of the Bishop Luffa School that students identified as evidence of the Christian nature of the school.

Students highlighted the 'interaction' between year groups, and the sense of support the older students gave the younger students. The sixth-formers were helping with RE revision sessions for Year 11; they were mentoring students in Key Stage 3; they were helping younger students to prepare for a national competition or organising lunchtime Christian Union sessions. It generated an atmosphere that students likened to a 'more family-type setting'. There was a general emphasis throughout the school on charity fundraising; that 'was just how the school works'. Students described it as like a continual process that made 'you feel like you are doing something good for everyone else'. One student reflected that a person's beliefs were unimportant, but that with this time and effort devoted to charity work 'it feels like you're doing things as if you were a Christian'.

The head teacher drew attention to the 'quality of care shown not just between pupils and staff but also between pupils'. He explained how this was rooted in the Christian ethos of the school with a reflection on the meaning of 'because' in the school mission statement. A few years previously the statement used to say, 'always our best **and** everyone matters'. However, in the regular review of the school vision, someone suggested that the 'and' needed to be replaced with 'because', the reasoning being that 'we try our best ... because in God's eyes everyone matters' (head teacher).

The way the people interact and the way that people act is quite in keeping with Christian morals and ideals, in the sense that people care about each other, they look after each other, the teachers are genuinely concerned about students. And I think that really shows through, and a lot of students have recognised that compared to other schools. (Student)

As part of the ethos you gain an understanding that when people help other people everyone can succeed. I think it is a better attitude, even if it does sound slightly clichéd. (Student)

We are explicit about being a Christian organisation and we say very clearly the reason why we have a motto, 'always our best because everyone matters' – everyone matters to us because everyone matters to God. That's why we aim for always our best and that's why it matters. (Head teacher)

Understandings of spiritual development

The climate established in Bishop Luffa, with a focus on openness to inquiry and care for each other, with space and time for reflection, contributed to the spiritual development of students. The establishment of such a climate in Bishop Luffa had enabled many students and staff to articulate clearly what spiritual development meant for them. Their responses focused on three interrelated aspects: an 'understanding of self'; developing in 'relationships' with other people; and a focus on developing in relation to God.

For a few adults, spiritual development for students was understood in terms of 'becoming more mature in their faith', in the context of a church school. But for the majority of students and staff the contribution made by the Bishop Luffa School was the provision of space and time to think about matters of faith, in a climate characterised by an openness – and an encouragement to question within a school community that prioritised the Christian concepts of compassion, forgiveness and reconciliation.

> **To be able to own their faith for themselves so that they're not just going to church because their parents drag them along but because they personally have a relationship with God through Christ.** (Staff)

> **I think that spiritual development is just like developing as a person, sort of knowing what you believe in, and it's all about discussing that.** (Student)

Chapter overview

- Providing space for reflection:
- Time for reflection and reconciliation
- 'Time for inquiry; a time to push the boundaries'
- Time to care 'because everyone matters'
- Understandings of spiritual development

Endnote

1. 'Spiritual spaces' is an approach set up to provide dedicated resources to support sixth-form tutors and students in having materials to facilitate a dedicated weekly time for 'spiritual space'. It was initially three staff – two teachers and a member of support staff (the librarian) – who put together the resources. We worked with a consultation group of sixth-form representatives. We now have a two-year rolling programme for the time sixth-formers are with us. It includes poetry, film clips, artwork, speeches to ponder, dilemma cards, in-class and more active out-of-class activities, e.g. using mirrors and copies of a palette of colours. Tutors have a resource file of samples and a door sign to use to try and avoid interruptions for those few minutes each week, which can often occur in busy school life. (Head of RE, Bishop Luffa School)

11

Implications of the research

This final chapter consists of two sections. In the first, Ann Casson highlights some implications emerging from the research that are of particular relevance for schools that want to have a positive influence on young people's spiritual development. The second comprises some closing reflections from Trevor Cooling on the place of spiritual development in the context of Christian-ethos secondary schools.

Section 1: Implications of the research investigation

This section is devoted to consideration of the main implications that arise from the research study. The case studies in this book illuminate the numerous ways in which these ten Christian-ethos secondary schools contribute to students' spiritual development and demonstrate that there are many factors that uniquely influence each individual.

1.   THE STUDENT PERSPECTIVE ON SPIRITUAL DEVELOPMENT

A question that the student research focus groups in all ten schools thoroughly enjoyed discussing was: 'What is spiritual development?' The responses generated provide an interesting insight into young people's awareness of what it means to be spiritual. The students' understanding fell into four distinct categories.

a.   The development of self: 'what you should be, what else you could be and how you need to respond to the world'.

b.   Community – a connection with other people: 'the person's own sense of who they are in their connection to each other'.

c.   A deepening of knowledge and understanding: being able to articulate an informed reasoned opinion on matters of faith and religion.

d.   A relationship with God: often spoken of in terms of getting closer to God and/or making a connection with God.

The original question underpinning the Ten Leading Schools research investigation was: 'What features in these ten Christian-ethos schools contribute to the positive spiritual development of students?'

One way to understand the contribution of the many features identified is to view them through the lens of these four categories above: self, community, knowledge, and a connection to God. These categories are interrelated. Indeed, they could be viewed as a virtuous spiral in so much as an influence in any one area will inevitably influence the others. In all ten schools, these categories are interwoven to create a holistic approach to spiritual development, but for ease of reference I will select a few examples to illustrate each category.

a.   The development of self

An integral element of spiritual development is knowing oneself and being able to be fully oneself. In fact, to be able to live one's life to its full potential is an essential aspect of spiritual development, rooted in John 10.10, 'I have come that they may have life and have it to the full'. Staff and students in all the schools stressed the importance of recognising young people as unique individuals who need support and encouragement to discern their hopes and aspirations in order to fulfil their God-given potential. For example, The John Wallis Academy and the Oasis Academy, Coulsdon demonstrate some of the key features that contributed to this area of spiritual development, such as a pastoral care system rooted in a Christian context, a school culture of care and nurture, the setting of high expectations and the prioritising of hope and aspiration. The story of Nottingham Emmanuel School highlighted how framing the spiritual development of self in terms of a journey provides a way for students to reflect on and influence their own spiritual development, and to support others on that journey.

b.   Community

People flourish within a community; being with others is essential to developing fully as a human being. Students and staff in all ten schools emphasised the importance of a sense of belonging to the school community and several shared examples of how relationships developed within this school had supported them in difficult times or spurred them on to achieve goals they had thought impossible. The story of the Bishop Justus School highlights the importance of hospitality and a welcoming atmosphere within the school community – a sense of belonging expressed in the little things of life, such as the 'hello' in the corridor and characterised by relationships of care for each other. In the Bishop Luffa School, the practice of restorative approaches, framed by the concepts of truth, forgiveness and reconciliation, contributes to a sense of a community that is inclusive and forgiving.

This sense of community extended beyond the immediate school community and was often expressed as a duty to care for others in the world, underpinned by an understanding that one's development as an individual is dependent on the flourishing of others. Several schools, such as Abbey Grange Academy and St Mary Redcliffe and Temple School, root their Christian ethos in the concepts of hope and justice; they actively raise awareness of issues of social justice in the local community and beyond and encourage students to be active in fighting injustice on behalf of the vulnerable.

c.   A deepening of knowledge and understanding

The third strand to emerge from conversations with students and staff was that spiritual development is about deepening knowledge and understanding of the spiritual dimension of life. Young people are curious about the big questions of life and wish to understand more about the nature of both the spiritual and of the religious and to work out what that means for their own lives and spiritual identity.

Archbishop Tenison's High School and The Blue Coat School both demonstrate the contribution that RE and collective worship programmes make when they seek to enhance questioning skills, and encourage students to interrogate concepts and to develop informed views and opinions about spiritual and religious matters. Students value the time to discuss, debate and ask questions; in many schools this time and space is found in RE and in collective worship. Throughout the ten schools there is a focus on developing theological literacy: for example, ensuring that all students can access and understand collective worship concepts, terms and practices. For those students who already had a basic knowledge, it is about challenging them to grapple with more complex theological concepts. The provision of opportunities for students to encounter the Christian scriptures in a holistic manner enables them to develop a deeper understanding of the Bible and to engage with the stories, the characters and the text itself, which is an important aspect of this deepening of knowledge and understanding.

d.   A connection to God

Within all these schools, students spoke of spiritual development as being about developing a 'connection with God'. In some cases, it was talking about developing an awareness of another dimension to life, a sense of awe and wonder, but for others, spiritual development was about working out their own relationship with God, or forming an opinion on the concept of God. A key feature found in these schools, which contributes to this aspect of spiritual development, is the presence of a prayerful culture. For example, in St Joseph's there is the visible practice of prayer by staff, students and leadership and an acceptance of the centrality of prayer by all within the community.

For the students, collective worship is an opportunity to develop this 'connection to God'. In all ten schools there were a variety of opportunities for collective worship, including the formal Eucharist, assemblies and form worship in a diversity of styles. There is an expectation that worship would happen regularly, be respected by all, and be engaging and relevant. The positive influence of prioritising, protecting and monitoring collective worship and of providing formal support for all staff who lead worship creates a culture where collective worship provides space for reflection. One consequence of this culture is the creation of a safe space within the whole of school for faith conversations, as seen particularly in the stories of the Bishop Justus School and The Blue Coat School.

2.   THINKING STRATEGICALLY AND ACTING DELIBERATELY

A major implication of this research study for those who wish to prioritise spiritual development in schools is that it cannot be left to chance. It is sometimes assumed that, in a Christian-ethos school, spiritual development will look after itself; the school does not need to do anything. A lesson learnt from this research is that to establish an environment in which spiritual development can flourish depends on its being prioritised at all levels, including governance and management. The features that contributed to spiritual development in these ten schools did not happen by chance, but are the result of decisions implemented after much deliberation and reflection. An example is the prioritisation and protection of morning worship, and consciously encouraging staff and students to role-model Christian values and practices. Areas identified where the schools had thought strategically and acted deliberately that had a positive influence on students' spiritual development included:

- The provision of opportunities for students to put 'faith into action'.

- Making of time and space for reflection in the everyday life of the school.

- The prioritisation of and a holistic approach to the spiritual development of staff and students in all aspects of school life – governance, teaching and learning, behaviour management, etc.

- An awareness and acknowledgement of the active agency of students.

a.   'Faith into action'

Spiritual development occurs in doing, in taking action. When students sought to identify the features that contributed to spiritual development in their school, they often framed their response in terms of what they or others did. Spiritual development is about making a difference in the world, putting beliefs into action. Many of the ten schools offer opportunities for students to engage in acts of service and be active supporters of charities, as seen in the case of Abbey Grange Academy. Here the Archbishop of York Young Leaders Award enables students to develop the talents needed to put 'faith into action' and actively encourage students to develop leadership skills in this area. Character education is an important element of several of the schools' contribution to spiritual development and it is understood by the students in terms of 'doing', of living out Christian values in the everyday. One feature that students highlighted was the Christian role models in their school; for example, in The John Wallis Academy students pointed to teaching staff or senior leaders as role models of Christian values.

b.   Time to reflect

An essential element underpinning all aspects that made a major contribution to spiritual development is the provision of the space and time to reflect; time to think about one's behaviour and beliefs. For students and staff, having time in school to process and reflect on the spiritual dimension of life is perceived to have a major influence on their ability to develop spiritually. Schools provided opportunities for reflection in teaching and learning, pastoral care, and in worship time. Some schools provide a 'sacred space', a chapel or a chaplaincy room where students and staff could come and sit in quiet and reflect.

c.   A holistic approach

One of the main findings of this research project was that each of the ten schools involved had a holistic approach to spiritual development. Even though in the case study Chapters I have highlighted one or two features of a particular school, each of these schools had an understanding that positive spiritual development happens in an environment where it is prioritised across all areas of school life. Spiritual development is not confined to any one part of the curriculum, nor to a specific time, nor is it just the responsibility of the Religious Education team, worship coordinator, chaplain or head teacher; rather, it is a whole-school responsibility that permeates the life of the community.

The nature and attitude of the staff population influences approaches to spiritual development. This study highlighted the importance that all ten schools give to ensuring all staff are willing to promote the Christian ethos of the school. Many of the schools stressed that the application process, the interview, induction and continuing professional development are key to selecting staff who are not only sympathetic to the school ethos but able to actively promote it. Many staff themselves shared stories of how they had deliberately chosen to work in a Christian-ethos school, or how working in such a school influenced their own spiritual development.

d.   An awareness of the active agency of students

This book has considered many features of ten schools that positively influence students' spiritual development. However, what cannot be forgotten is that the schools do not operate in a vacuum; the nature of the student population inevitably influences the form that spiritual development may take within a school. Young people are not a blank slate, they bring with them into school attitudes and opinions and, most importantly, are active in their own development of a spiritual identity.

One of the main implications of this research study is that the context in which each of the schools operated is key. The ten schools had developed and implemented programmes, policies and strategies dependent upon the nature of the school, the location, the staff and the student population. It is essential for schools to be aware of students' existing levels of spiritual development. It might appear that this is to some extent determined by admissions criteria, but these criteria do not reveal students' experience, knowledge and understanding of, or their attitudes to, the spiritual dimension of life. What the research in these schools highlighted is that when schools are aware of individual students' needs in the area of spiritual development, a more positive, profound and relevant contribution can be made.

One final but very important implication of this research study is the need to recognise and acknowledge the active agency of the young people involved. In the course of the visits to the Ten Leading Schools, many students participated in focus groups. The questions they discussed were the same as those given to the adults in the research project, such as: What is spiritual development? What in this school contributes to students' spiritual development? As can be seen from the case studies, the young people's answers were deep and thoughtful. The spiritual dimension of life is of interest to many young people and they are, each in their own unique way, working out their spiritual identity. As one of the interviewees reminded us, it is important to remember that the students are not only leaders and role models of the future, they are leaders and role models among their peers today. There is a need to listen to the views and opinions of the young people, to understand their experiences of faith and to facilitate them being active agents in their own spiritual development and that of others.

Section 2: The Place of Christian faith in spiritual development

1.   CONFIDENTLY CHRISTIAN

Christian-ethos schools are central to the provision of education in the UK, with over a third of the state-funded system falling within this category. As our study of ten of these schools from the secondary sector shows, they are highly variable, ranging from those that serve challenging local areas where there is little explicit Christian presence to those that offer a vibrant local Christian community, an education where Christian faith is explicit. In all their forms, Christian-ethos schools are popular with parents.

However, there is significant opposition to their presence, with the British Humanist Association leading the way by employing a full-time staff member to campaign for the withdrawal of state funding from all such schools. The main basis of this opposition lies in the assumption that the schools are sectarian and out to convert rather than to offer an education that promotes the flourishing of all pupils and contributes to the creation of a healthily diverse society. They are perceived as designed to serve the churches' need to recruit new members and are portrayed as the last desperate attempt to keep the churches from imminent decline. In this view, these schools are seen as toxic rather than as beneficial to society. Reading the stories of our ten schools should be enough to convince that this is a false picture. This study gives every reason for those working in Christian-ethos schools to be confidently Christian in their work – with one proviso.

One of the oft-voiced justifications for state funding for Christian-ethos schools has been rights-based. The argument goes that Christians are entitled to run schools because Britain is a Christian country and because Christian parents are entitled to the education that they want for their children. There is truth in this argument in that Christians clearly have rights like every other citizen, but it can be unhelpful both in its portrayal of the Christian motivation for being involved in education and in its implication of the place that Christians see themselves as having in wider society. It makes people think that being a Christian is all about protecting a privileged position for the church in society. Given the statistics of the decline in church attendance and the increasing influence of non-religious worldviews in Britain, this is politically untenable. But more worryingly, it misrepresents the nature of Christian mission.

At the heart of Jesus' mission is the notion of gift, not entitlement; servanthood not domination. Consequently, the proviso to the rights argument is that gift, not entitlement, frames the way that Christian-ethos schools understand their contribution. They have the immense privilege of being able to offer society the gift of an education that promotes 'life in all its fullness' (John 10.10) for pupils. The recent vision statement from the Church of England's Foundation for Education Leadership[1] (*Deeply Christian, Serving the Common Good*) transcends that tension by showing how the Christian vision of life in all its fullness is a blessing for all people, not just for Christians. It is an education that promotes pupils' spiritual development so that if they are Christians they are prepared for a life of making gifts to others; and if they are not themselves Christians they experience the gifts that Christ offers to all in a way of living that is wholesome. Threading through this vision is the notion that whatever our religious and non-religious commitments we learn to live well together in the midst of our diversity. It is on this basis that we can be confidently Christian about offering Christian-ethos schools in modern Britain. We seek only the right to serve society from the resources of the Christian faith, not the right to dominate society and to defend the Church against the threat of change. Our ten schools exemplified this aspiration in ten different ways.

2.   THE NATURE OF CHRISTIAN-ETHOS EDUCATION

Central to the gift that Christ offers is a vision of life lived as God intended and a desire to see young people develop as people of character in line with that vision. This manifested itself in two particular ways in the ten schools that participated in this research.

a.   Values and virtues

For many years, schools have emphasised the importance of values education. Of late, this has nuanced to an emphasis on virtue development. The main reason for this change is that values education can stop with intellectual consideration of debates about values, whereas virtues education focuses on the person that you are becoming. The Tom Hanks film *Sully* illustrates the difference. Chesley Sullenberger III (Sully) is the pilot who landed a passenger plane on the Hudson River in New York in 2009 following a catastrophic bird-strike that disabled all the plane's engines. Everyone survived. Sully is purported to have said of the incident: 'One way of looking at this might be that for 42 years, I've been making small, regular deposits in this bank of experience, education and training. And on January 15 the balance was sufficient so that I could make a very large withdrawal.' Anglican theologian Tom Wright comments on this in his book *Virtue Reborn*,[2] saying that Sully's experience illustrates the importance of consistent attention to the daily development of character. The significant aspect of the Sully story was his ability to respond as a person in a challenging situation by making wise decisions and being of exemplary character. It was not his knowledge of the US Airway's manual on dealing with engine failure that saved 155 lives but his ability to respond out of who he was. What counted were the virtues that he had developed over many years of his education, not just the values discussed in that education. Our ten schools were all engaging with this focus on character as an integral component of spiritual development.

b.   The importance of inclusivity

A second theme that emerged from our ten schools was the concern to offer an experience of spiritual development that was inclusive. The danger for Christian-ethos schools is that they become two-tier environments where pupils and staff feel that there is an inside circle of people who are Christians and an outside circle of those who have not made such an explicit commitment. None of our schools manifested this approach. Rather, their concern was to offer an experience of spiritual development within a Christian-ethos education where everyone flourished and felt affirmed. There was a consistent emphasis on the importance of learning to live well together in the context of significant diversity in wider society.

However, one big question that arises from our study is exemplified by the comment of an atheist friend of mine. On hearing about an approach developed within a Christian-ethos school, he remarked that the problem with it was that it was not Christian. His point was that he liked the approach because he thought it resulted in quality education for the pupils, and if he, as an atheist, liked it it could not therefore be Christian. His assumption was that for anything legitimately to be describable as Christian it had to be *uniquely* Christian – something one would only find in Christian-ethos schools. If he is correct, then it is clearly difficult to see how much of what has been described in our ten schools can be called Christian. The values and virtues promoted and the desire to be inclusive are often found in other schools.

This argument, however, makes three errors.

- What makes the approaches in these schools Christian is not their uniqueness, but the source on which they draw. For example, the O-Zone for autistic students in the Oasis Academy, Coulsdon could have been set up by any school. However, in their case, it was inspired by the biblical account of Jesus' care for the vulnerable. The foundation, inspiration and motivation for actions matter, not just the actions themselves.

- That leads to the second point: that actions should not be judged in isolation from their context. One thing that stands out from our ten schools is their practice of prayer and their dependence on the Bible. When a school like the Oasis Academy seeks to be inclusive it is doing so within a context that is framed by a distinctively Christian understanding of the world. The school is not just affirming a shared human value but is rather living out a Christian value, which others also affirm, but not for the same reasons.

- Finally, sometimes the Christian underpinning does break out into a distinctive emphasis. Two clear examples are a principal who prays openly, in The John Wallis Academy, and an approach to RE that champions theological literacy, in Archbishop Tenison's School.

This emphasis on the significance of the underpinning Christian framework for these schools leads to one further observation, namely the significance of the Religious Education programme in a Christian-ethos school. If the pupils are to appreciate the Christian grounding of the virtues espoused by the school they will need to be introduced to that grounding. Hence the importance of high-quality approaches like *Understanding Christianity*,[3] which was sponsored by the Church of England and helps pupils to think theologically.

The practice of prayer has emerged as a particular theme in our ten schools. This may be controversial in modern society, where the offer to pray with someone is sometimes interpreted as a hostile intrusion and occasionally leads to Christians in the caring professions losing their jobs. This is sad because, as we have seen in this research, the practice of prayer can be a supportive and affirming activity for all, irrespective of their personal faith. However, for prayer to be experienced as a hospitable gift rather than a hostile intrusion, two things are necessary. First, we need to move away from the secularist notion that prayer is inevitably an offensive intervention; this is a matter of religious literacy. We all need to learn how to receive from those who are religiously different from us without taking offence. Second, those offering prayer need to be highly sensitive to the needs and feelings of those they pray with and not behave in an intrusive manner; this is a matter of Christian hospitality.[4]

3.   A NOTE FOR NON-RELIGIOUS SCHOOLS

This book recounts the findings of an intensive research study of ten Christian-ethos secondary schools. However, the findings should be of interest to other schools, since all schools are required to promote the spiritual development of their pupils. In particular, the following insights are relevant:

● The need for senior leaders to think strategically and act deliberatively about spiritual development. It will not just happen because the school has a policy statement tucked away in a file somewhere.

● Making context-appropriate decisions is crucial to success. In particular, decisions made about policy and practice in spiritual development have to be sensitive to the background and nature of the school's pupils and staff.

● Most of what has been highlighted in our ten schools can be adapted by schools that do not share their Christian ethos. Part of the thrill of our richly diverse society is that we can all learn from each other, even though we may come from very different starting points.

Endnotes

1. https://www.churchofengland.org/media/2532968/gs_2039_-_church_of_england _vision_for_ education.pdf

2. *Virtue Reborn*. London: SPCK, 2010.

3. http://www.understandingchristianity.org.uk

4. For further discussion of these theological issues see Trevor Cooling with Beth Green, Andrew Morris and Lynn Revell, Christian Faith in English Church Schools: *Research Conversations with Classroom Teachers*, Oxford: Peter Lang, 2016.

Appendix

The quantitative research strand

Introduction

The quantitative strand of this project was shaped by three theoretical considerations and by two related research traditions.

The first theoretical consideration was rooted in an examination of the central place given to the notion of 'ethos' in the very title of the project. As a research team we were invited to examine the ethos of Christian schools. Ethos is an elusive term, but also a term of wide relevance for understanding school distinctiveness and school effectiveness. The qualitative strand of the research explored ethos in its broadest sense as experienced, observed and recorded by Ann Casson as the researcher who immersed herself within the life of the ten schools.

Building on several of Leslie J. Francis' earlier studies, the quantitative strand argued that one core factor in shaping the ethos of a school is the overall set of values, attitudes and beliefs of the students. Listening to the students, it is argued, provides the clearest and deepest insight into the ethos of the school. It is the overall set of values, attitudes and beliefs of students that shape the environment into which a new student to the school is welcomed and by which that student may be shaped. The quantitative strand focused specifically on exploring the values, attitudes and beliefs of the students.

The second theoretical consideration was rooted in a measurement approach to values, attitudes and beliefs. The measurement approach is concerned with identifying broad ideas and devising short, sharp survey questions to exemplify and to capture these ideas. This approach can be expressed in two ways. Sometimes an area of values, attitudes or beliefs can be profiled by giving attention to the individual items. Sometimes an area of values, attitudes or beliefs can be profiled by developing scale scores that are measuring the students' responses to the underlying idea. Both of these two ways are employed in the quantitative strand. Samples of the results are included in each chapter on the ten schools. These give an indication of the ethos generated by the students in each school.

The third theoretical consideration was rooted in the discussion of the theological motivations underpinning Christian-ethos schools as set out in the opening chapter to this book. In that chapter we distinguished between Jesus' concern with two different styles of learning communities: the twelve disciples, whom he nurtured deeply, and the crowd of 5,000 whom he served generously. Christian-ethos schools are also concerned with two styles of activity, nurturing students from the Christian community and serving students who may not regard themselves as followers of Christ.

Some church schools place their major emphasis on nurturing children from churchgoing families. Other church schools place their major emphasis on serving a diverse local neighbourhood. This difference is reflected primarily in the admissions profile of schools. As a consequence of differences in admissions there may also be considerable differences in the overall set of students' values, attitudes and beliefs. The quantitative strand set out to test this hypothesis.

The first of the two research traditions drawn on by the quantitative strand came into play in the first year of the project. This strand was shaped in a series of books by Leslie J. Francis, beginning with *Youth in Transit* (1982) and reshaped by *The Values Debate* (2001). This research tradition has identified a set of values domains and developed sets of survey questions to capture students' responses to these domains. The quantitative strand drew on this research tradition so that the values of students in the ten Christian-ethos schools could be set alongside recent data gathered from students in schools without a religious character.

The second of the two research traditions drawn on by the quantitative strand came into play in the second year of the project. This strand was shaped by work initiated by Leslie J. Francis in 1974 with the development of the *Francis Scale of Attitude toward Christianity*. This is a 24-item scale concerned with students' affective responses to God, Jesus, Bible, church and prayer. Since its construction in 1974 this survey has been translated into over 20 languages and used in over 300 published studies. The quantitative strand of our research drew on this research tradition so that the trajectory in scores of attitude toward Christianity from Year 7 to Year 11 in the ten Christian-ethos schools could be set alongside established data collected from a variety of schools over the past 40 years.

Assessing values

In year one of the project all students in Year 9 and Year 10 classes of the ten Christian-ethos schools were invited to complete the *Francis Values Survey*. All told, 2,942 students from these ten schools participated. These data were used to test two research questions. The first research question set the responses of the 2,942 students attending our ten Christian-ethos schools alongside the responses of 10,455 students attending 55 schools without a religious character. The research question is this: Is there an overall difference between the ethos generated by students in our Christian-ethos schools and by students in schools without a religious character?

The second research question compared the overall responses of students within two of the Christian-ethos schools. The two selected represented the schools with the greatest proportion of students from Christian backgrounds and the school with the least proportion of students from Christian backgrounds. The former school (which we will call school A) had responses from 194 students. The latter school (which we will call school B) had responses from 302 students. The research question is this: Is there a difference between the ethos generated by students in the two schools?

Both research questions were tested against eight of the values domains covered in the *Francis Values Survey*: namely religious beliefs, church and society, science and religion, sexual morality, substance use, social concerns, school, and personal well-being. The data demonstrated that the major differences occurred not so much between Christian-ethos schools and schools without a religious character, but between church schools that experience the Church's mission in education differently. This finding will be illustrated by taking sample questions from each of the eight values domains.

The set of questions on religious beliefs included three items on belief in the persons of the Holy Trinity. The three items concerned with the Holy Trinity demonstrate that there was a much higher level of belief in the three persons of the Holy Trinity among students attending Christian-ethos schools than among students attending schools without a religious character. In Christian-ethos schools 48% believed in God (compared with 26%), 46% believed in Jesus Christ (compared with 23%), and 41% believed in the Holy Spirit (compared with 18%). The real variation, however, came within the Christian-ethos schools. In school A, 79% believed in God, compared with 23% in school B, and similar differences emerged in respect of belief in Jesus (83% and 19%) and belief in the Holy Spirit (78% and 20%).

The set of questions on church and society included two items on the place of religious rites of passage (marriage and baptism). There was comparatively little difference between the proportions of students who wanted to get married in church attending schools without a religious character (51%) and attending Christian-ethos schools (57%). Within our two schools the variation was greater. Within school A, 69% of students wanted to get married in church, compared with 49% in school B. The item concerning baptism was a stronger discriminator among the different schools than the item concerning marriage. While 31% of students attending schools without a religious character wanted their children to be baptised, christened or dedicated in church, the proportion rose to 49% within Christian-ethos schools. While 29% of students in school B wanted their children to be baptised, christened or dedicated in church, the proportion rose to 78% in school A.

The set of questions on science and religion included two items on the origins of the universe. The belief that God made the world in six days of 24 hours was endorsed by a higher proportion of students in Christian-ethos schools than in schools without a religious character (23% compared with 11%). In school B the proportion was similar to that in schools without a religious character (10%). In school A, endorsement of the belief that God made the world in six days of 24 hours was much higher, at 47%. On the other hand, acceptance of the general narrative of evolution was higher and with little difference between students attending schools without a religious character (49%), Christian-ethos schools (48%) and school B (49%). In school A, the proportion of students endorsing the general narrative of evolution fell to 32%.

The set of questions on sexual morality included items on sex before marriage, on sex under the legal age, and pornography. Students attending Christian-ethos schools recorded a more conservative attitude than students in schools without a religious character. Thus, 16% of students in Christian-ethos schools agreed that it is wrong to have sex before you are married, compared with 9%; 46% agreed that it is wrong to have sex under the legal age, compared with 30%; 46% agreed that pornography is wrong, compared with 33%. Overall, students attending school A reported a more conservative position on these issues compared with students attending school B. Thus, 31% of students in school A agreed that it is wrong to have sex before you are married, compared with 8% in school B. In terms of agreeing that it is wrong to have sex under the legal age, the proportions were 55% and 46%; and agreeing that pornography is wrong the proportions were 68% and 43%.

The set of questions on substance use included items on smoking cigarettes, getting drunk and using ecstasy. On all three issues, students in Christian-ethos schools were slightly more conservative than students in schools without a religious character. Thus, in Christian-ethos schools, 60% considered it wrong to smoke cigarettes compared with 53%; 29% considered it wrong to get drunk compared with 20%; and 66% considered it wrong to use ecstasy compared with 63%. The responses were also higher in school A than in school B. Thus, in school A, 72% considered it wrong to smoke cigarettes compared with 51%; 38% considered it wrong to get drunk compared with 29%; and 79% considered it wrong to use ecstasy compared with 67%.

The set of questions on social concerns included items on concern related to the developing world, to terrorism and to nuclear war. The item on concern about poverty in the developing world revealed higher concern among students in Christian-ethos schools (73% compared with 63%). The highest level of concern was found in school A (80%) and the lowest level of concern was found in school B (51%). The item on concern about the risk of terrorism revealed higher concern among students in Christian-ethos schools (61% compared with 55%). The highest level of concern was found in school A (66%) and the lowest level of concern was found in school B (52%). The item on concern about the risk of nuclear war revealed higher concern among students in Christian-ethos schools (46% compared with 42%). In school A, the proportion stood at 46% compared with 39% in school B.

The set of questions on school included two items designed to assess overall attitudes toward school. The first item revealed no great difference in terms of overall happiness in school. Thus, the proportions of students who agreed that they are happy in their school stood at 70% in schools without a religious character, 69% in Christian-ethos schools, and 68% in both school A and school B. The second item, however, revealed a less negative attitude toward school in the Christian-ethos sector. While 51% of students in schools without a religious character said that school is boring, the proportion fell to 43% in Christian-ethos schools. The view that school is boring was endorsed by 31% of students in school A and 39% of students in school B.

The set of questions on personal well-being included items concerned with positive well-being and items concerned with negative well-being. An example of positive well-being focused on purpose in life. A slightly higher proportion of students in Christian-ethos schools feel their life has a sense of purpose, 71% compared with 67% in schools without a religious character. The proportions, however, rose to 82% in school A, but remained at 66% in school B. Examples of negative well-being focused on suicidal thoughts and on self-harm. The variation on the negative well-being items was much less. One in five of the students across all four samples reported that they have sometimes considered taking their own life (19% to 21%), and one in four across the four samples reported that they have sometimes considered deliberately hurting themselves (24% to 25%).

Assessing attitude toward Christianity

In year two of the project all students in Years 7, 8, 9, 10 and 11 of the ten Christian-ethos schools were invited to complete the *Francis Scale of Attitude toward Christianity*. All told, 6,538 students attending the ten schools participated in the survey. These data were used to test two research questions. The first research question explored the pattern of attitude scores across all ten schools and looked for differences in terms of sex, age and the individual school. The second research question explored whether the connection between age and mean attitude scores varied from school to school. Each of these two research questions will be explored in turn.

Table 1

Attitude toward Christianity scores by sex, age and school

	Mean	SD
By sex		
Male	78.9	26.4
Female	81.7	25.1
By school year		
Year 7	90.1	23.9
Year 8	83.7	24.1
Year 9	80.3	24.9
Year 10	74.3	26.2
Year 11	72.0	25.8
By school		
School 1	98.2	21.4
School 2	89.2	24.2
School 3	85.1	25.6
School 4	84.4	22.7
School 5	81.9	26.4
School 6	77.9	24.5
School 7	77.3	25.1
School 8	75.4	23.7
School 9	69.2	25.2
School 10	64.6	24.0

Table 1 addresses the first research question and shows the mean attitude scores by sex, by age, and by individual school. Before being able to interpret these scores it is necessary to know how the scores have been calculated. *The Francis Scale of Attitude toward Christianity* comprises 24 short and clear statements. Here are two examples: Prayer helps me a lot; God means a lot to me. Each statement is rated by the students on a five-point scale, as follows: disagree strongly (1), disagree (2), not certain (3), agree (4), and agree strongly (5). The lowest score a student can record on the scale is 24 (i.e. 24 x 1), and the highest score a student can record on the scale is 120 (i.e. 24 x 5). A midway score may be seen as 72 (i.e. 24 x 3).

Three clear findings emerge from Table 1. The first finding is that female students record a more positive attitude toward Christianity than male students. The difference is not that great but it is statistically significant and totally consistent with the findings of international research using the same instrument. Women hold a more positive attitude toward Christianity than men and this is widely reflected by the gender imbalance in the majority of church congregations.

The second finding is that attitude toward Christianity declines progressively during the years of secondary schooling. This decline was first monitored using the *Francis Scale of Attitude toward Christianity* in a study conducted in 1974 and was replicated by studies conducted in 1978 and 1982, and by a number of subsequent studies. Much of the earlier work was drawn together in Francis' book *Drift from the Churches* (1996). Even in these ten Christian-ethos schools the overall decline from 90.1 to 72.0 over these five year groups is quite severe.

The third finding is that there are really strong differences in the mean scores of attitude toward Christianity within these ten Christian-ethos schools. The difference is between 98.2 in the school recording the most positive attitude toward Christianity and 64.6 in the school recording the least positive attitude toward Christianity. If attitude toward Christianity can be taken as a measure of Christian ethos, the students within these two contrasting schools (the highest scoring and the lowest scoring) are experiencing learning within quite different environments. In this sense no consistent assumption can be made about the levels of positive Christian affect among the student body within Christian-ethos schools.

Table 2

Attitude toward Christianity scores by age across schools

	Year 7	Year 8	Year 9	Year 10	Year 11
School 1	103.2	100.9	103.0	96.4	88.2
School 2	100.3	93.6	88.5	85.3	78.7
School 3	96.9	85.8	84.3	74.7	79.7
School 4	95.1	86.4	80.2	74.1	71.4
School 5	92.7	86.1	82.0	76.5	80.7
School 6	91.4	84.3	74.3	70.2	64.6
School 7	86.0	81.4	76.4	67.5	64.7
School 8	81.5	77.5	80.7	72.8	70.7
School 9	70.7	63.2	64.2	65.1	60.5
School 10	69.0	72.8	72.1	62.8	68.1

Table 2 addresses the second research question by exploring whether the decline in attitude toward Christianity scores with age is consistent across all ten Christian-ethos schools. The clear finding from this table is that school 1 stands apart from the others in the sense that attitude scores in Year 9 are no lower than attitude scores in Year 7. There are two theories that could account for the distinctive performance of school 1.

The first theory is that this school had brought together in Year 7 a group of students who hold a positive attitude toward Christianity and that this positive attitude generated a self-sustaining environment in which positive Christian affect could flourish. The mean attitude score in Year 7 stood at 103.2, the highest among all ten Christian-ethos schools. The second theory is that this school managed its Christian education activities in a way that actively maintained and supported positive Christian affect among the students. Theory one attributes the support to sustain positive attitude toward Christianity to the student body, while theory two attributes that support to the strategy of the school.

Adjudication between these two theories may not be easy. A clue may, however, be given by examination of school 2. School 2 also began in Year 7 with a group of students who held an attitude score almost as high as in school 1 (100.3 compared with 103.2). School 2 was not, however, able to sustain this high score into Year 8 and Year 9. This finding, then, lends greater weight to theory two, namely that the distinctive performance in school 1 may be attributed to the Christian education strategy implemented in that school. If this theory is correct, it means that schools can make a difference to their students' attitude towards Christianity by the strategies they adopt to spiritual development.

What may need to be noted, however, is that the school identified as school 1 in the study concerned with assessing attitudes towards Christianity is the same as that identified as school A in the study concerned with assessing values. It may simply be easier for Christian-ethos schools that are admitting students from Christian homes to support a culture of Christian ethos than for Christian-ethos schools that are setting out to serve Christ by offering quality education for a diverse and secular local catchment area.

References
Francis, L. J. (1982), *Youth in Transit: A profile of 16–25 year olds.* Aldershot: Gower.
Francis, L. J. (2001), *The Values Debate: A voice from the pupils.* London: Woburn Press.
Kay, W. K., and Francis, L. J. (1996), *Drift from the Churches: Attitude toward Christianity during childhood and adolescence.* Cardiff: University of Wales Press.